中国国家汉办重点规划教材

Chinese Paradise
—The Fun Way to Learn Chinese

Teacher's Book 3

刘富华　王　巍

周芮安　李冬梅　编著

邵　壮　译

目 录 CONTENTS

UNIT SIX BIRTHDAY & FESTIVALS

Introduction

Chinese Paradise is a series of textbooks for an elective course of elementary Chinese for children in English-speaking countries. There are 15 volumes altogether: 6 volumes of Student's Book, 6 volumes of Workbook, 3 volumes of Teacher's Book both in Chinese and in English.

I. Teaching objectives

Students will:

1. be able to understand and speak some simple Chinese sentences;
2. be able to sing some Chinese children's songs and recite children's rhymes and simple poems;
3. acquire some basic knowledge of Chinese characters, such as the basic strokes and stroke order, and be able to write some simple Chinese characters;
4. gain a preliminary understanding of some of the Chinese culture.

II. Principles of compiling

1. Learner-oriented with scientific arrangement of the contents
   Language teaching is integrated with presentation of cultural information, games and hands-on activites in view of some special characteristics of children in English-speaking countries, such as being lively, enjoying moving around in class, and being interested in making handicrafts and playing games. In order for students to learn Chinese and understand China through perceptual activities, language teaching is treated as the foundation while cultural information and games and hands-on activities as the supplements. Multi-media teaching resources such as Teacher's Book, audio cassettes, CDs and CD-ROMs are accompanied with the textbooks catering to the need for different teaching means.

Teaching of the language points and training of the language skills are arranged in accordance with the rules of Chinese acquisition as a second language. The text, vocabulary and grammar are taught in a scientific, rational and progressive way. Teaching of Chinese characters, words and expressions and sentences are conducted through lively and interesting activities. In brief, students learn Chinese in an enjoyable and relaxing atmosphere, which well represents the compiling principles of this series— teaching by pleasurable means and learning in entertainment.

2. Presenting knowledge of interest to children
Taking the arrangement of the topics for situational dialogues as an example, the selection of the topics is based on their practical application in communication and scientific methods of language teaching, as well as some special characteristics of children, such as liveliness and curiosity. Some common communicative topics selected include greeting, expression of thanks, inquiry and invitation etc., and other topics favored by children, such as travel, entertainment, sports and pets etc.

In view of the liveliness of children, entertaining and hands-on activities are provided in the Student's Book and Workbook, for example, making handicrafts and stick-on pictures etc. Thus, the integration of language teaching, cultural introduction and game playing has been achieved.

III. Contents of teaching
1. Teaching of vocabulary
The decision on the quantity of the vocabulary included in this elementary course was made in consultation with *HSK Guidelines for Chinese Words and Characters* developed by the Department of Chinese Proficiency Test (HSK), China's National Office for Teaching Chinese as a Foreign Language (NOTCFL) and the syllabus of the Chinese language for primary schools in English-speaking countries such as Australia and so on. The total number of words is about five hundred (500). Those words listed in the Student's Book are required ones, while the rest of them presented in

the Teacher's Book with *pinyin* and English translation are supplementary ones.

2. Teaching of Chinese characters

Learning Chinese characters is difficult for students of English-speaking countries. In order to help students overcome the difficulty in learning Chinese characters, this course has made the following arrangements:

(1) The aim of teaching Chinese characters is to help students develop an interest in Chinese characters. Students are not required to write every Chinese character. It is sufficient for them to be able to recognize and read simple Chinese characters and have a preliminary understanding of the rules of character writing.

(2) One or two Chinese characters (mainly the pictographic characters) are chosen from each lesson in the Student's Book to help students understand the origin and evolution of Chinese characters and recognize and read them with the help of pictures.

(3) In the Workbook, various activities to practise Chinese characters, for instance, cutting out, sticking stick-on pictures, coloring characters and adding strokes etc., are designed to avoid the dullness and tediousness in practising writing Chinese characters.

(4) A set of cards of Chinese characters with illustrations is available in the Student's Book to help the teacher explain the Chinese characters.

3. Teaching of *pinyin*

Two special features of this series is the tone illustrations and the alphabets of *pinyin* presented with color cartoon animals. Some nursery rhymes, ancient poems and tongue twisters are supplied to make the teaching of *pinyin* interesting and entertaining. The tones actually used in daily conversations are marked to show the alternation of tones in the flow of the language. Specific information can be found in The Scheme for the Chinese Phonetic Alphabet attached to the Teacher's Book.

4. Teaching of grammar

More than forty basic sentence patterns and grammar points are selected based on the topics in the Teacher's Book. Detailed descriptions are given to each grammar point. In view of the receptive ability of children, the part of grammar in this course is only prepared for teacher's reference and need not be explained in class.

5. Introduction to culture

To facilitate language teaching, some information on the Chinese culture interested by children, such as *wushu,* holidays and animals etc., are provided. The information also helps students gain a preliminary understanding of the Chinese physical geography, social life, history and culture and enhance their enthusiasm to learn Chinese.

6. Games and hands-on activities

Some games and hands-on activities of Chinese cultural characteristics are designed and presented in the last section of each lesson of the textbook, for example, kicking shuttlecocks, practicing Chinese *Kung fu,* making dumplings, and making paper-cuts and kites etc.

IV. Stylistic rules and layout

1. There are 6 volumes of Student's Book at 3 levels, each of which consists of twelve lessons. Stylistic rules and layout are as follows:

   1) Can you say?

   It includes two parts: a situational dialogue and new words. New words that are of the same color as the words and expressions in the dialogue can be used in substitution exercise.

2) Can you try?

This is an interactive game which helps students practise with the teacher the sentence patterns and the new words in "Can you say?" by means of a game.

3) Do you know?

This is the part of cultural introduction, in which illustrations of the Chinese culture are presented with a brief introduction. A question is usually included also, and students can find the answer to the question in the teacher's explanation.

4) Learn to read.

It is the part of Chinese *pinyin* in Volume 1 of Student's Book, and that of nursery rhymes, ancient poems, riddles and tongue twisters in Volume 2 and Volume 3.

5) Let's talk.

It is a short dialogue presented only in Volume 3 of Student's Book, which can be performed by students to review the lesson.

6) Learn to write.

This is for practising Chinese characters. In Volume 1 and Volume 2 of Student's Book detailed explanation about a Chinese character (two characters in some lessons) is given in each lesson, while in Volume 3 two or three Chinese characters are taught in each lesson.

7) Let's do it.

This is the game or hands-on activity. Simple and interesting Chinese traditional games and hands-on activities such as making handcrafts are provided. Most of these games and activities are related to the language teaching and cultural information given in this lesson.

8) Let's sing.

Chinese songs are usually supplied in the latter part of the second lesson of each unit.

9) Story time

A story can be found in the latter part of the second lesson of each unit. Comic strips are used to help students review the learned lessons. Students may come across some new sentences in this part, but they are not required to master them.

10) Review

In the final part of every three units a review page with stickers is presented to help students review the main sentence patterns of these three units. Furthermore, a list of vocabulary is attached to the Student's Book.

2. Workbook

Workbook, an exercise book of *Chinese Paradise*, is accompanied with the Student's Book. There are altogether 6 volumes of 3 levels. Each volume consists of 12 lessons and each lesson contains 6 – 8 exercise problems. Besides, an additional exercise is provided as homework in the Workbook of level 3. Exercises of each lessen are divided into four sections: *Pinyin*, Chinese Characters, Words and Expressions, and Dialogue. Furthermore, sticker pages and exercises of tracing the characters are attached to each Workbook.

3. Teacher's Book

There are altogether 3 volumes of Teacher's Book both in Chinese and in English. Color stickers are attached to the back of each volume for the teacher to reward students.

Apart from all mentioned above the following teaching accessories are also available:

1) A pack of teaching aids which include small items of Chinese cultural characteristics and related to teaching, for instance, a mask of the Handsome Monkey King, a kite, a skipping rope, a shuttlecock, paper-cuts, and a Chinese knot etc. After the instruction of each book is completed the student with the most color stickers can be given a present from the package as a reward.
2) CD accompanied with the book as a borus.
3) CD-ROM.
4) Cards of Chinese alphabets.
5) Cards of words and expressions from Student's Book.
6) Wall pictures.

V. Allocation of time for teaching

The arrangement of the contents in this series allows for flexibility in view of the fact that there are not sufficient number of class hours for Chinese teaching in English speaking countries and different number of class hours are allocated to Chinese teaching in different schools. Schools with fewer number of class hours may skip some games and hands-on activities, while schools with more can provide more activities by using the Teacher's Book and the supplementary materials accompanied with it.

The suggested number of class hours allocated to teaching of each volume is as follows:

Volume 1: four class hours for each lesson;

Volume 2: five class hours for each lesson;

Volume 3: six class hours for each lesson.

We hope you will find *Chinese Paradise* helpful in your Chinese teaching.

The compilers

UNIT ONE   SEASONS & WEATHER

Lesson 1

SPRING IS COMING.

Focus: The Seasons

Objective: Patterns: 春天来了。

真暖和！

Vocabulary: 春天，夏天，秋天，冬天，冷，
热，暖和，凉快，来，了，真

Chinese Characters: 春，天

Culture: China's Climate

Teaching aids:　(1) four pictures which represent spring,
summer, autumn and winter
(2) materials for making a pinwheel: small
wooden sticks, a cardboard, a drawing
pin
(3) a wall map of China

STUDENT'S BOOK

Review and introduction

Ask the class the current season in English and ask some students "你喜欢什么季节？" (which season do you like?), then stick the season pictures on the board according to students' answers.

▲ 1. Can you say? (CD)

Translation of the dialogue

Spring is coming. It's *warm*.

Translation of the substitutes

①*summer,hot* ②*autumn,cool* ③*winter,cold*

Supplementary words:

潮湿	cháoshī	humid
干燥	gānzào	dry

Grammar:

(1) 春天来了。(Spring is coming.)

"了" is a modal auxiliary here, which is placed at the end of a sentence, to indicate the state of affairs has changed or is going to change. For example:

秋天来了。(Autumn is coming.)

下雨了。(It is raining.)

(2) <u>真暖和</u>！

"真" is an adverb expressing emphasis. It means "very, really" and is often used in colloquial Chinese. For example:

真好吃！(It is very delicious!)

真好看！(It is really beautiful!)

◆ 2. Can you try?

Steps: (1) Prepare four vocabulary cards with "春天", "夏天", "秋天" and "冬天".

(2) Invite some students to come to the front of the class to perform. The teacher then holds up a vocabulary card such as 冬天 and says aloud "冬天来了".

(3) The performers immediately give the relevant actions. For example: to shiver as if it is cold.

(4) The other students then utter "真冷！" in chorus according to the performance.

◆ 3. Let's talk. (CD)

Steps: (1) Characters introduction: Xiaolong, Jack. Explain the dialogue in English according to the pictures of the plot in STUDENT'S BOOK.

(2) Students listen to the CD, then read aloud in different roles and do imitating practice.(five minutes for preparation)

(3) Students come to the front of the class to perform in groups and the teacher makes comments. Groups which perform excellently will be awarded colored stickers.

Translation of the dialogue:

Xiaolong: Autumn is coming.

Jack: The autumn in Beijing is very beautiful!

Xiaolong: Do you like autumn?

Jack: Yes, it is cool.

▲▼ 4. Do you know? (CD-ROM)

China's Climate

China's climate varies widely in different regions because of its vast territory and complicated topography. At the very northern end of China summers are short and winters are long and very cold. Whereas Hainan Island, located at the southern end of China, has no winter and is hot all year round. A humid climate envelops most of Chinese southeastern coastal cities throughout the year while the Qinghai-Tibet Plateau is perennially covered with snow. Therefore, while traveling all over China during one season, you may still be able to enjoy various sceneries of different seasons.

Game:

Prepare four vocabulary cards with "冷", "热", "暖和" and "凉快". Then ask students to stick the vocabulary cards on the corresponding parts of a map of China.

▲▼ 5. Learn to read. (CD, CD-ROM)

An Ancient Poem

Hymn to the Goose

Honk, honk, and honk,
With upward neck thou to the sky loudly sing.
Thy white feathers float on the water green,
Thy red webs push the crystal waves with a swing.

天

In ancient times "天" with its original meaning "head" or "the top of a man's head", resembles the obverse of a standing man especially emphasizing the figure of a man's head. Now "天" with its extended meaning "sky above the head" can generally refer to nature. In recent times a day and night can also be called "一天", e.g., "今天" and "明天"(tomorrow) etc..

7. Let's do it. (CD-ROM)

Make a Pinwheel

Steps: (1) Prepare a piece of square cardboard.

(2) Fold the opposite angles along two diagonals.

(3) Cut the diagonals with scissors inwards to the places 2cm away from the center.

(4) Bend each angle clockwise towards the center.

(5) Fix the four angles with a drawing pin on a wooden stick.

(6) Walk briskly or run outdoors against the wind raising the pinwheel, the pinwheel will spin.

8. Let's sing. (CD, CD-ROM)

Where is the Spring

Where is the spring, where is the spring?

The spring is right in the kids' eyes.

Hare are the red flowers, and there the green grass.

Still there are little orioles that can sing.

Li, li, li....

Li, li, li....

Still there are little orioles that can sing.

Still there are little orioles that can sing.

WORKBOOK

♦ 1. Write and say.

Steps: (1) Students trace and write the Chinese characters according to the given order of the strokes.

(2) Students read out the four seasons in Chinese and interpret.

♦ 2. Look and stick.

Steps: (1) Students read the thermometer according to their own country's reading either in Fahrenheit (F) or Centigrade (C) . Note: conversion table:

$$F = 9 \times C \div 5 + 32$$
$$C = (F - 32) \times 5 \div 9$$

(2) Students tell cold, hot, warm, cool, then choose the corresponding stickers from the sticker pages and put them on the blanks.

♦ 3. Color and match them.

Steps: (1) Students match the word to its *pinyin* and picture.

(2) Students color spring, summer, autumn and winter with suitable colors as directed by the teacher.

♦ 4. Find, circle and write.

Steps: (1) Instruct the class to read the words and explain their meanings.

(2) Ask Students to choose words related to weather

learned in this lesson and circle them with crayon.

(3) Ask students to write down the corresponding *pinyin* on the lines according to the pictures below.

Answers: ①lěng ②rè ③nuǎnhuo ④liángkuai

◆ 5. Listen, choose and color them. (CD)

Steps: 1. Students listen to the CD and choose the correct pictures.

2. Students color the pictures.

CD script:

Qiūtiān lái le, zhēn liángkuai !
① 秋天 来 了, 真 凉快!

Xiàtiān lái le, zhēn rè !
② 夏天 来 了, 真 热!

Dōngtiān lái le, zhēn lěng !
③ 冬天 来 了, 真 冷!

◆ 6. Choose, draw and say.

Steps: (1) Ask students to imagine their favorite season, then write them in the corresponding frames.

(2) Ask students to draw a picture of their favorite season including a self-portrait with clothes of the present season in the frame.

(3) Invite students to come to the front of the class to talk about their drawing. Students who do excellently will be awarded colored stickers.

◆ 7. Complete the dialogues.

Step: Read the dialogues. Then complete them according to the pictures.

Answers:

① 喜欢。 春天 很 暖和。
Xǐhuan. Chūntiān hěn nuǎnhuo.

② 不 喜欢。夏天 很 热。
Bù xǐhuan. Xiàtiān hěn rè.

③ 喜欢。 秋天 很 凉快。
Xǐhuan. Qiūtiān hěn liángkuai.

④ 不 喜欢。 冬天 很 冷。
Bù xǐhuan. Dōngtiān hěn lěng.

◆ 8. Look and say using "真……!"

Steps: (1) Students read the pictures, and try to say sentences according to the words given below the pictures.

(2) Elicit students' answers, and correct them when necessary.

HOMEWORK

Ask students to find out the climates of the countries they are interested in by Internet and give a brief report at the next class session.

Lesson 2

WHAT'S THE WEATHER LIKE TODAY?

Focus: The Weather

Objective: Pattern: 今天天气怎么样？
Vocabulary: 晴天，阴天，下雨，下雪，刮
风，天气，怎么样
Chinese Characters: 风，雨
Culture: The Origin of the Kite

Teaching aids: (1) a coat, a pair of sunglasses, a umbrella, a
hat, a pair of gloves, etc.

(2) two self-made head ornaments
representing "晴天" and "阴天"
respectively

(3) a kite

(4) a piece of colored paper and a pair of
scissors for cutting paper snow flakes

9

STUDENT'S BOOK

Review and introduction

(1) Review the words of the four seasons"春","夏","秋" and "冬",and the weather conditions such as"冷","热", "暖和" and "凉快"etc. using the vocabulary cards.

(2) Open the windows and ask in English: "What's the weather like today?" Then take out the two head ornaments with "晴天" and "阴天" and let the class choose which one to wear.

◆ 1. Can you say? (CD)

Translation of the dialogue

What's the weather like today?

It *rained*.

It's *sunny* today.

Translation of the substitutes

①*snow*　②*windy*　③*cloudy*

Supplementary words:

打雷	dǎ léi	thunder
闪电	shǎndiàn	lightning
多云	duōyún	cloudy

Grammar:

今天天气怎么样? (What's the weather like today?)

"怎么样" is an interrogative pronoun used as a predicate for inquiring the state of affairs. It is equivalent to English word

10

"how" or "what". For example:

明天天气怎么样？(What's the weather like tomorrow?)

我们去公园怎么样？(How about going to the park?)

⬧ 2. Can you try?

Steps: (1) Put the coat, sunglasses, umbrella, hat and gloves on the table.

(2) Prepare vocabulary cards ("下雨"，"下雪"，"刮风"，"晴天" and "阴天").

(3) Invite some students to come to the front of the class, and face the rest of them holding up a vocabulary card. Ask the rest of them to utter in chorus, e.g. "下雨了。" The students at the front of the class immediately get the relevant item (for example, pick up a umbrella and open it). Find out who is the fastest.

(4) Review words about cold, hot, warm and cool in Lesson 1 at this time.

⬧ 3. Let's talk. (CD)

Steps: (1) Characters introduction: teacher, Annie. Ask students to listen to the CD, and read aloud in different roles and do imitating practice. (prepare for 5 minutes)

(2) Divide students into groups and ask them to perform in front of the class and make comments. The groups which perform well will be awarded colored stickers.

Translation of the dialogue:

Teacher: What day is today?

Annie: It's Tuesday.

Teacher: What's the weather like today?

Annie: It snowed, very cold.

Teacher: How about tomorrow?

Annie: It will be a sunny day.

◆ **4. Do you know?** (CD-ROM)

The Origin of the Kite

Kites were invented in China over 2000 years ago. One day a clever man saw a hawk hovering in the sky for a long time. Inspired by what he had seen he made a "wooden kite" according to the appearance of the hovering hawk. The early kite was very big and was used for carrying men or for military purpose. Later, with the invention of paper people began to make smaller kites with paper and bamboo sticks. As the method for kite making became simpler, everyone could make their own kites. As a result, flying kites was developed into a popular activity for sports and recreation and has been passed down to us.

Do you know that the invention of kites has once inspired the invention of plane? Nowadays more and more people like kite flying around the world. Weifang, a Chinese city, was chosen as the world capital of kites on April 1, 1988. Since then the (world) Kite Festival has been held annually in Weifang.

◆ **5. Learn to read.** (CD, CD-ROM)

A Riddle

It looks like thousands of threads,

It looks like millions of threads,

But it can't be seen while falling into water.

6. Learn to write. (CD-ROM)

雨

"雨" originally means rainwater. In inscriptions on bones or tortoise shells "雨" resembles the shape of raindrops. Therefore Chinese characters with the radical "雨" are associated with astronomical phenomena such as cloud, rain and snow etc. and also have the extended meaning of falling from the sky, e.g., "雷"(thunder), "雪"(snow), "雾"(fog), etc..

7. Let's do it. (CD-ROM)

Flying a Kite

Steps: (1) Take out a kite and briefly explain how to make a kite to the class.

(2) Take the class to a big grassland or square on a windy day.

(3) Unwind the string from the spool, throw up the kite and run against the wind regulating the angle and height of the kite to allow it to fly high up into the sky.

8. Story time. (CD, CD-ROM)

① How wonderful today's weather is!
② So high! So beautiful!
③ Look! Everybody likes me!
④ It's raining!
⑤ Help!

WORKBOOK

▲▼ 1. Stick and write.

Steps: (1) Ask students to read the Chinese characters and tell the meaning of them.

(2) Ask students to choose the correct stroke stickers from the sticker pages and paste them according to the given order of the strokes.

(3) Ask students to practise writing the Chinese characters in the given frames.

▲▼ 2. Circle out the correct *pinyin* for each character.

Steps: (1) Students read each Chinese character according to the indication.

(2) Students choose the correct *pinyin* for each character, and then read aloud and interpret.

▲▼ 3. Listen, draw and color them. (CD)

Steps: (1) Students listen to the CD. Then draw oppropriate items for the figures.

(2) Color the finished drawings.

CD script:

Jīntiān qíngtiān.
① 今天　晴天。

Xià yǔ le.
② 下 雨 了。

Xià xuě le.
③ 下 雪 了。

Guā fēng le.
④ 刮 风 了。

4. Look and match them.

Steps: (1) Ask students to look at the pictures and match according to the weather in the pictures.

(2) Invite students to answer.

5. Look and answer.

Steps: (1) Say "今天怎么样?" and then point to the pictures on the left or right to ask students to answer according to the pictures.

(2) Repeat the same exercise with another question: "昨天天气怎么样?"

6. Recall the weather for last week.

Steps: (1) Ask students to recall the weather for last week.

(2) Ask students to fill each of the blank on the calendar paper with an appropriate weather sign.

(3) Ask students to make a summary of last week's weather and say it out.

7. Draw and say.

Steps: (1) Instruct students to forecast the weather for the following day according to today's weather.

(2) Students draw a colored picture of the weather for the following day according to their imagination. Local symbolic buildings should be included in the picture.

(3) Students describe the weather of the following day according to their drawing.

8. Make a snow flake. (CD-ROM)

Steps: (1) Take out the colored paper, a pair of scissors and a pencil.

(2) Fold the paper and draw lines according to the pattern on the picture. Then cut out the pattern.

(3) Unfold the paper, a six-angled snowflake is ready.

HOMEWORK

Ask students to color the cover of their kite and find out which one is the most colorful and most resembles a butterfly (remind the students to pay close attention to the symmetry of the butterfly).

Lesson 3

CAN YOU SWIM?

Focus: Sports

Objective: Patterns: 你会游泳吗？

我不会。

Vocabulary: 乒乓球，棒球，网球，篮球，游泳，滑冰，会，打

Chinese Characters: 网，球

Culture: *Taijiquan* ——The art of *Taiji*

Teaching aids: (1) sports equipment related to this text (such as table tennis, basketball, tennis etc.)

(2) a pair of table tennis bats, a table tennis net or a piece of rope, a scoreboard

STUDENT'S BOOK

Review and introduction

(1) Check students' homework by asking them to show their kite drawings. Choose the best one and award the student a colored sticker.

(2) The teacher and students talk about the seasons and weather. Then the teacher asks students their favorite sports of the present season and writes them on the board.

(3) Ask each student in English "Can you...?" to introduce the sentence pattern of this lesson.

▲ 1. Can you say? (CD)

Translation of the dialogue

Can you *swim*?

I can *swim*.

I can't.

Translation of the substitutes

①*play table tennis* ②*play baseball* ③*play basketball/*
④*play tennis* ⑤*skate*

Supplementary words:

滑板	huábǎn	skateboard
排球	páiqiú	volleyball
足球	zúqiú	football
橄榄球	gǎnlǎnqiú	rugby

Grammar:

你会游泳吗? (Can you swim?)

"会" is a modal verb which comes before a verb expressing being able to do or knowing how to do something. It can be used independently to answer a question. Its negative form is "不会". For example:

我会说汉语。(I can speak Chinese.)

我不会打篮球。(I don't know how to play basketball.)

"会" can also be used as a verb which comes before a nominal object expressing an understanding of something or familarity with something. For example:

我会汉语。(I know Chinese.)

她会什么？(What docs shc know?)

▲▼ 2. Can you try?

Steps: (1) Stick six vocabulary cards about sports in a row on the board.

   (2) Stand before the first card (e.g., "棒球") and ask "谁会打棒球？" Students with the answer "会" immediately come to the front and stand in a line.

   (3) Count the students and write the number on the board just below the card "棒球". The students then return to their seats.

   (4) stand at the next card and continue until all the six sports are completed. Students may come forward as many times as they are able to play the six different sports. The teacher makes a summary and asks each sports group: "你们会打棒球吗？" The students in each group answer: "我们会打棒球。", "我们会打乒乓球。" etc..

   (5) Then lead the class to find out the most popular sports.

◆ 3. Let's talk. (CD)

Steps: (1) Students listen to the CD and then follow the teacher to read aloud.

(2) The teacher explains the dialogue. Students then read aloud in different roles and do a role play.

(3) Students perform in groups and the teacher makes comments. Groups which perform well will be awarded colored stickers.

Translations of the dialogue:

Annie and Jack:　Hello!

Xiaolong:　Hello!

Xiaolong:　Where are you going?

Annie and Jack:　We are going to play tennis. Will you go with us?

Xiaolong:　No, I don't know how to play tennis. I can play table tennis.

◆ 4. Do you know? (CD-ROM)

Taijiquan —— The Art of *Taiji*

Taijiquan is one of the Chinese martial arts practised by both ancient and modern Chinese for maintaining health and for self-defense. Doing *Taijiquan* requires a quiet and relaxed mind, calm and subtle movements, and a combination of gentle and hard movements. Practising *taijiquan* also requires the concentration of the mind and a perfect combination of breath and movement to achieve the goal "深shen, 长chang, 习xi, 静jing" (referring to the breathing being as deep, long, relaxed and calm as possible). It is believed that doing *taijiquan* frequently will benefit a person's cerebrum, nerve and internal organs. In China there are many people who practise *taijiquan* daily. As one Chinese saying goes: "Practising *taijiquan* everyday keeps the doctor away!"

♦ 5. Learn to read. (CD, CD-ROM)

Two Proverbs
Sow beans and you get beans.
A word once spoken cannot be taken back even by a team of four horses.

♦ 6. Learn to write. (CD-ROM)

网

"网" originally means "a tool used for catching fish, birds or animals." In inscriptions on bones or tortoise shells, "网" is a net in the middle with wooden sticks on both sides. The name "网球" comes from a net in the middle of a court.

♦ 7. Let's do it. (CD-ROM)

A Table Tennis Match

Table tennis, a national sport in China, is one of the favorite sports of the Chinese. Playing table tennis not only promotes good health but also enhances a person's physical reaction and mental agility. Furthermore, compared with other sports table tennis requires lesser space, simple equipment and is not restricted by the weather. These factors account for the growing popularity of table tennis not only in China but also in many other countries.

Steps: (1) Lead the class to set up a table for table tennis.
　　　　　　If a proper table is unavailable, join a few small tables

together to form one and put a net in the middle of it.

(2) Either explain or let students watch the CD-ROM to learn the rules of the game. Here are some rules:best three of five games or best four of seven games, and 11 scores for each game. After every 2 points scored the receiving player becomes the server, and the server will lose a point if the ball misses the opponent's court.

(3) Organize students to practise serving balls (in pairs or two pairs).

(4) Organize a match, and serve as the umpire and the scorekeeper.

(5) The winners will be awarded colored stickers.

8. Let's sing. (CD, CD-ROM)

A Doll Is Dancing with a Little Bear

A doll is dancing with a little bear, dancing and dancing, yee-yee-oh.

A doll is dancing with a little bear, dancing and dancing, yee-yee-oh.

A doll is dancing with a little bear, dancing and dancing, yee-yee-oh.

A doll is dancing with a little bear, dancing and dancing, yee-yee-oh.

WORKBOOK

▲ 1. Join the dots and write.

Steps: (1) Ask students to try to read the characters and tell the
meaning of them.

(2) Ask students to trace the Chinese characters written in
dotted line.

(3) Ask students to match the other two Chinese characters
in the circles of the other pair.

▲ 2. Match them.

Steps: (1) Ask students to try to read the word "打", and
understand its meaning as well as its part of speech.

(2) Ask students to match the verb "打" with appropriate pictures.

(3) Read out the correct verb-object collocations.

Answers: dǎ   bàngqiú / wǎngqiú / lánqiú / pīngpāngqiú
　　　　　　打　棒球 ／ 网球 ／ 篮球 ／ 乒乓球

▲ 3. Write *pinyin*, match and color them.

Steps: (1) Studens mark the *pinyin* for each Chinese character
vocabulary card.

(2) Students look at the colored pictures, then match them
with the words according to the meaning of the pictures.

(3) Students color the dotted pictures.

◆ 4. Listen and tick. (CD)

Steps: (1) Ask studens to listen to the CD twice, and choose the correct pictures.

(2) The teacher asks questions and students retell what they have heard.

CD script:

Jiékè   huì dǎ   pīngpāngqiú.
① 杰克 会 打　乒乓球。

Xiǎolóng   bú huì   yóuyǒng.
② 小龙　 不 会　游泳。

Wǒ   xǐhuan   dǎ   lánqiú.
③ 我　喜欢　打　篮球。

Answers: ①A　②B　③A

◆ 5. Find and say.

Steps: 1. Ask studens to find out the correct sports pictures at the right along the lines starting from the figure paintings at the left.

2. Students write the names of the sports on the lines below the pictures with *pinyin* or Chinese characters.

Answers:

huá bīng   dǎ wǎngqiú   dǎ pīngpāngqiú
安妮：滑 冰 方方：打 网球　圆圆：打乒乓球

yóuyǒng   dǎ bàngqiú
杰克：游 泳 小龙：打 棒球

◆ 6. Complete the dialogue.

Steps: (1) Ask students to look at the pictures, and complete the dialogue.

(2) Ask students for their answers and then give the correct answers.

Answers:

Nǐ huì dǎ pīngpāngqiú ma?
杰克：你 会 打 乒乓球 吗？

Bú huì.
小龙：不 会。

Nǐ huì dǎ lánqiú ma?
杰克：你 会 打 篮球 吗？

Huì, wǒ xǐhuan dǎ lánqiú.
小龙：会，我 喜欢 打 篮球。

Hǎo! Wǒmen qù dǎ lánqiú.
杰克：好！ 我们 去 打 篮球。

7. Ask, stick and say.

Steps: (1) Students ask the classmates beside them (a boy and a girl) in Chinese "你喜欢什么季节、衣服、天气、运动和食物？"

(2) Students who are asked look for the stickers related to their answers in the sticker pages and put them on the frames.

(3) The teacher invites students to explain in Chinese their frames.

HOMEWORK

Ask students to color the *Taiji* picture with their favorite colors using their own imagination according to the cultural content of this text. Choose the best five works and put them on the blackboard at the next class session.

UNIT TWO   SPORTS & HOBBIES

Lesson 4

Focus: Hobby

Objective: Patterns: 我喜欢唱歌儿，你呢？
Vocabulary and Phrases:画画儿，唱歌儿，跳舞，看电影，玩儿电子游戏，听音乐，呢
Chinese Characters: 画，电
Culture: Chinese Calligraphy and Painting

Teaching aids: (1) a writing brush, ink, watercolors, a piece of used newspaper or Xuan paper (high quality rice paper for traditional Chinese painting and calligraphy)
(2) two paper cups, a handful of rice, a piece of adhesive tape

Review and introduction

(1) Check students' homework and choose the best five works and put them on the board.

(2) Go over the patterns of the last lesson such as "我会游泳。" and words about sports with the vocabulary cards.

(3) Introduce the topic of the new lesson by using words about sports: e.g., take out a vocabulary card and say "我喜欢游泳。", then point to a student and ask: "你呢?"

◆ 1. Can you say? (CD)

Translation of the dialogue

I like *singing*, and *you*?
I like *dancing*.

Translation of the substitutes

① *draw pictures* ② *play electronic games* ③ *see movies*
④ *listen to the music*

Supplementary words:

看动画片 kàn dònghuàpiàn   see cartoon movies
做运动   zuò yùndòng   do sports

Grammar:

我喜欢唱歌儿，你呢?

"喜欢" is a verb which can take a noun as its object, e.g., "我喜欢狗"; "喜欢" can also take a verb as its object, e.g., "我

喜欢唱歌儿".

"呢" is a modal auxiliary which can be put after a noun or pronoun to compose an interrogative sentence inquring "how". For example:

我很好，你呢?（=你好吗?）

I'm fine, and you? (=How about you?)

我喜欢吃饺子，你呢?（=你喜欢吃什么? 你喜欢吗?）

I like eating dumplings, and you? (=What do you like to eat? Do you like it?)

我去学校，你呢?（=你去哪儿? 你去吗?）

I go to school, and you? (=Where are you going? Will you go too?)

2. Can you try?

Steps: (1) Lead the class to sit in a circle indoors or outdoors on the grass.

(2) Randomly put the vocabulary cards of this lesson in the circle.

(3) Pick up a card and speak aloud to student A on the right: "我喜欢××，你呢? A?"

(4) Student A immediately goes to the center of the circle to pick up his favorite card and answers "我喜欢××。" Then he asks student B on his right the same question "你呢?" Student B answers and this continues to the next student.

(5) The student who hesitates or gives a wrong answer walks around the circle once while reading his favorite card, and the game goes on.

3. Let's talk. (CD)

Steps: (1) Characters introduction: Fangfang, Annie. Ask students

to listen to the CD, then read aloud the dialogue in different roles and practise through role playing.

(2) Students perform in groups. The groups that perform well will be awarded colored stickers.

Translation:

Fangfang: What 's your hobby?

Annie: I like drawing, how about you?

Fangfang: I don't like it, I like playing electronic games.

Annie: How about Jack?

Fangfang: He likes skating.

♦ 4. Do you know? (CD-ROM)

Chinese Calligraphy and Painting

Chinese calligraphy and painting are art forms with a very long history. Chinese Calligraphy is an ancient art which came into being with the emergence of the Chinese characters. It is not only a method of writing characters but also an art of representing a person's temperament, character and sentiment through lines and structures. With the development of the history of calligraphy many calligraphy styles such as Zhuan, Li, Cao, Xing, Kai etc., as well as the various schools of calligraphy appeared.

Chinese painting, an embodiment of special aesthetic culture and custom of the Chinese, differs greatly from Western painting. Chinese painting places an emphasis on affinity of spirit rather than the appearance or the differentiation of brilliance and color. Generally speaking Chinese painting falls roughly into three broad categories: figure painting, landscape painting and flower-and-bird painting.

Currently the materials of the stationery (writing brush, ink, Xuan paper, ink stone) used in creating calligraphy and Chinese painting differ greatly. In the past the writing brush had a bamboo handle and the brush made from the fine hair of the rabbit or weasel was called "毛笔"; "墨" was a kind of jet-black ink made from natural minerals; "纸"was paper made from rice differing from ordinary paper in its great ability to absorb moisture; "砚", a container for grinding ink, was made of stones and its shape may differ from each other. All of these were called "four precious stationery of study" in ancient China.

▲▼ 5. Learn to read. (CD,CD-ROM)

A Tongue Twister

On top of the green pine, resting a dragonfly.

The dragonfly is resting, motionlessly resting,

The dragonfly is resting motionless on top of the green pine.

▲▼ 6. Learn to write. (CD-ROM)

▲▼ 7. Let's do it. (CD-ROM)

Draw a Simple Traditional Chinese Painting: Swallow

Steps: (1) Prepare a writing brush, ink, watercolors and a piece of paper (or used newspaper).

(2) Demonstrate briefly the correct method of holding a Chinese writing brush, grinding ink, dipping ink and wielding the brush.

(3) Draw the head and the back of the swallow with darker black ink. Draw the wings and the tail with black ink. Draw the chest with lighter black ink. Then draw the red neck and the black eyes. Finally draw the beak with deeper ink.

(4) On the reverse side of the painting write your name, the date and time on the bottom left corner.

▲ 8. Story time. (CD, CD-ROM)

① What do you go in for?

② I like singing.
   Wonderful!

③ I like drawing.

④ I can swim.
   I can play basketball.

⑤ How about you, little bear?
   I ...

⑥ He likes sleeping!

▲ 1. Write.

Steps: (1) Ask students to look at the pictures and think about the required Chinese characters that need to be written.

(2) Ask students to complete the two "田" with missing strokes to match the pictures.

⬍ 2. Find and write.

Steps: (1) Lead students to read the nouns and noun phrases, and
then ask students to guess their meanings.

(2) Ask students to find the object for each verb.

(3) Check their answers and correct them if necessary.

Answers:

huà huàr　　　tīng yīnyuè　　kàn diànyǐng
①画 画儿　②听 音乐　③看　电影

wán diànzǐ yóuxì　　chàng gēr　　　tiào wǔ
④玩儿 电子 游戏　⑤唱　歌儿　⑥跳　舞。

⬍ 3. Match them.

Steps: (1) Students read aloud the *pinyin*.

(2) Students find out the Chinese character, English
translation and the picture for each *pinyin*.

⬍ 4. Look and answer. (CD)

Steps: (1) Point to the pictures, read part A and ask questions.

(2) Students look at the pictures and answer the questions.

Answers:

Ānni xǐhuan chàng　gēr.
① 安妮 喜欢 唱　歌儿。

Xiǎolóng xǐhuan huà huàr.
② 小龙　喜欢 画 画儿。

Dìdi xǐhuan wánr diànzǐ yóuxì.
③ 弟弟 喜欢 玩儿 电子 游戏。

32

5. Listen and stick. (CD)

Steps: (1) Ask students to listen to the CD and find out the required musical instruments and tools for the persons in the picture.

(2) Students find the correct stickers in the sticker pages and put them in the right places.

(3) Award students who complete it with correct colored stickers.

CD script:

Fāngfang xǐhuan chàng gēr.

① 方方　喜欢　唱　歌儿。

Ānni xǐhuan tiào wǔ.

② 安妮　喜欢　跳　舞。

Jiékè xǐhuan huà huàr.

③ 杰克　喜欢　画　画儿。

Xiǎolóng xǐhuan tīng yīnyuè.

④ 小龙　喜欢　听　音乐。

Míngming xǐhuan wánr diànzǐ yóuxì.

⑤ 明明　喜欢　玩儿　电子　游戏。

6. Answer the questions according to the picture.

Steps: (1) Ask students to read aloud the statement and the questions.

(2) Students find out the answers according to the picture.

Answers:

Bàba bù xǐhuan hē kělè.

① 爸爸　不　喜欢　喝　可乐。

Gēge xǐhuan yóuyǒng.

② 哥哥　喜欢　游泳。

Māma xǐhuan kàn diànshì.

③ 妈妈 喜欢 看 电视。

Dìdi xǐhuan dǎ pīngpāngqiú.

④ 弟弟 喜欢 打 乒乓球。

 **7. Make a shaker.** (CD-ROM)

Steps: (1) Prepare two paper cups of the same size and a handful of rice.

(2) Pour the rice into the cups, then place the cups mouth to mouth and tape it with adhesive tape.

(3) Draw (or watercolor) pictures and write a name on the surface of the cups.

(4) Shake it after class.

 **HOMEWORK**

This is a homework for groups: first, ask students to find out their hobbies through group discussion; then get students to draw their self-portraits and their hobbies on the paper; finally ask the group leaders to collect the pictures and compile them into a picture book. An exhibition will be held at the next class session and the teacher will give comments and awards.

Lesson 5

I WANT TO BUY CHOCOLATE.

Focus: Shopping

Objective: Patterns: 你要买什么?

我要买巧克力和饼干。

Vocabulary: 巧克力，饼干，冰淇淋，糖，薯片，汉堡包，三明治，要，买，和

Chinese Characters: 买，和

Culture: Western Fast Food in China

Teaching aids: (1) vocabulary cards about food, drink and stationcry lcarncd bcforc

(2) food items related to the snacks in this lesson and a salesperson's apron

(3) chopsticks, peanuts

Review and introduction

(1) Check students' homework: "Make a book" and invite students to come to the front to display their works in groups. Students point to their self-portraits and say "我喜欢…" as a review to the previous lesson on hobbies.

(2) Dress up as a salesperson and take out the prepared materials and then ask the class to guess the topic of this lesson as an introduction.

1. Can you say? (CD)

Translation of the dialogue

What do you want to buy?

I want to buy *chocolate* and *biscuits*.

Translation of the substitutes

①*ice cream* ②*hamburger* ③*sandwich* ④*candy* ⑤*chips*

Supplementary words:

香肠	xiāngcháng	sausage
鸡蛋	jīdàn	egg
口香糖	kǒuxiāngtáng	chewing gum
比萨饼	bǐsàbǐng	pizza

Grammar

(1) 你要买什么？

"要" is an auxiliary verb which expresses the willingness to do something. Generally speaking it is not used to answer questions on its own.

For example: 你要去哪儿？(Where do you want to go?)

我要吃饺子。(I want to eat dumplings.)

Besides, "你要买什么？" is a very common expression used by salespersons to welcome a customer in China. It is the same as "May I help you?" or "What can I do for you?"

2. 我要买巧克力和饼干。

"和" is a conjunction which usually joins pairs of nouns, noun phrases and pronouns for expressing coordination. "和" is normally placed just before the last noun or phrase if there are three or more nouns and phrases.

For example: 我吃饼干和薯片儿。(I want to eat biscuits and potato chips.)

我有书、笔和本子。(I have books, pens and notebooks.)

⬆⬇ 2. Can you try?

Steps: (1) Join the class tables together. Spread out the vocabulary cards of the foods from this lesson and the vocabulary cards of the drinks and stationery from the lessons learned before on the table. Have students sit around the tables.

(2) Dress up as a salesperson and ask a student: "你要买什么，A？" Student A answers immediately and the other students try to touch the corresponding card as quickly as they can. The student who touches the card first takes it.

(3) Continue to ask the other students the same question one by one until all the cards have been taken. The student who has the most cards will be given a food item as a reward.

3. Let's talk. (CD)

Steps: (1) Characters introduction: Annie, Fangfang. Ask students to listen to the CD and then read aloud in different roles and do a role-play.

(2) Students perform in groups. The teacher then gives comments and rewards.

Translation script:

Fangfang: Where are you going, Annie?

Annie: I am going to the supermarket.

Fangfang: I am going to the shop. What do you want to buy, Annie?

Annie: I want to buy a hamburger, and you?

Fangfang: I want to buy a bag and a pencil.

Annie & Fangfang: Good-bye.

4. Do you know? (CD-ROM)

Western Fast Food in China

China is well known as "a nation for eating and drinking". Although Chinese dishes are famous for their dazzling varieties and tastes, western fast food has become increasingly popular especially with the younger generation. Mcdonald's and KFC have enjoyed a tremendous success in catering to the Chinese since they came to China in the late 1980s and these fast food restaurants have spread over most of the major cities in the country.

Why are the hamburgers and French fries so popular with young Chinese? According to a survey some of the reasons are: good service, clean, tidy and comfortable environment, game and playing areas, and attractive gift toys for children. Besides the young can also find a place to study and have birthday parties there. Teenagers are never bored with the food though their parents disapprove them having too much fried food. It seems hard to believe but the Mcdonald's and KFC stores are fully packed with people during weekends!

5. Learn to read. (CD, CD-ROM)

A Riddle
A house with a rough surface,
A bed-curtain with red color,
Under which live white and chubby babies.

6. Learn to write. (CD-ROM)

买

"买" in ancient Chinese means to get shells from a net. "贝" (shell) was used as a currency by the Chinese in ancient times for buying and selling goods. "买" now means the use of money to buy whereas "卖" means the opposite.

7. Let's do it. (CD-ROM)

A Chopstick Game—a Match of Picking up Peanuts

Chopsticks have existed in China for over 3000 years. In ancient times the Chinese ate food with their hands. However after the discovery of fire they initially did not know how to handle hot food. Therefore sticks were used to help with the food and eventually the skill of handling food with sticks was perfected. This was the origin of the chopsticks. Using chopsticks is simple, versatile, and convenient. Chopsticks are ideal for food such as noodle, chafing dish and dumpling. Today more than 1.5 billion people use chopsticks all over the world.

Steps: (1) Learn the correct way of using chopsticks.

(2) Divide the students into pairs and have a game of picking up peanuts with chopsticks. The student who picks up the most peanuts in one minute will be the winner.

(3) Find out who is the best in hand 119 chopsticks by.

8. Let's sing. (CD, CD-ROM)

A Song from a Newspaper Boy

La-la-la,la-la-la, I'm a little newspaper boy.

Start my work in the early morning.

One newspaper, another newapaper,

Today's news is really good.

And you can get two newspapers only for one coin.

WORKBOOK

1. Write.

Steps: (1) Students read the Chinese characters.

(2) Students trace the dotted strokes according to the given orders of the strokes.

(3) Students practise the Chinese characters in the given frames, and then count the number of strokes and put the results in the brackets.

♦ 2. Find out and write.

Steps: (1) Find out the corresponding *pinyin* according to the
given phrases.

(2) Write down the *pinyin* above the Chinese characters.

Answers:

shǔpiànr   bīngqílín   hànbǎobāo táng

①薯片儿 ②冰淇淋 ③汉堡包 ④糖

qiǎokèlì   bǐnggān

⑤巧克力 ⑥饼干

♦ 3. Match them.

Steps: (1) Students try to read the new words on the left.

(2) Students match the pictures to their translations.

♦ 4. Read, draw and say.

Steps: (1) Lead students to read the names of the foods in the
picture of the supermarket.

(2) Ask students to choose five of their favorite foods and
draw them in the shopping cart.

(3) Students color and read the names of their favorite
foods aloud.

♦ 5. Listen, tick and color them. (CD)

Steps: (1) Students listen to the CD twice, and then choose the
correct pictures.

(2) The teacher asks question and students color the correct
pictures.

CD script:

Ānni yào mǎi kělè.
① 安妮 要 买 可乐。

Jiékè yào mǎi hànbǎobāo.
② 杰克 要 买 汉堡包。

Xiǎolóng yào mǎi táng.
③ 小龙 要 买 糖。

Míngming yào mǎi shǔpiànr hé guǒzhī
④ 明明 要 买 薯片儿 和 果汁。

6. Repeat and expand the sentence.

Steps: (1) Read aloud the first sentence showing how to expand it.

(2) Then invite students one by one to expand the sentence and tell them to pay attention to the place where "和" is put.

7. Complete the dialogue.

Step: Students read the dialogue according to the pictures and then complete it.

Answers:

Xiǎolóng, nǐ hǎo!
安妮：小龙，你 好！

Nǐ hǎo! Ānni!
小龙：你 好，安妮！

Nǐ qù nǎr?
安妮：你 去 哪儿？

Wǒ qù shāngdiàn.
小龙：我 去 商店。

Nǐ yào mǎi shénme?
安妮：你 要 买 什么？

Wǒ yào mǎi bǐ hé běnzi.
小龙：我 要 买 笔 和 本子。

HOMEWORK

Ask each student to conduct a survey among 6 to 10 classmates to find out three most popular foods. At the next class session determine the three most popular foods from the surveys and announce it to the class.

UNIT THREE SHOPPING

Lesson 6

Focus: Asking the Price

Objective: Patterns: 一斤苹果多少钱？

五元。

Vocabulary: 苹果，梨，香蕉，西瓜，菠萝，

多少，钱，元，斤

Chinese Characters: 苹，果

Culture: Ancient China's Calculator — the Abacus

Teaching aids: (1) number cards 0 ~ 9

(2) fruits or fruit cards as many as possible

(3) a salesperson's apron and an abacus

STUDENT'S BOOK

Review and introduction

(1) Check students' homework and find out "the three most favorite foods of the class".

(2) A student dresses up as a salesperson and asks the teacher with the words learned from the previous lesson: "你要买什么?" The teacher points to a card and answers: "我买××。" The teacher then asks: "一斤××多少钱?" and writes the price on the board allowing students to guess the meaning of the sentence as an introduction to the new lesson.

♦ 1. Can you say? (CD)

Translation of the dialogue

A: How much is half a kilo of *apples*?

B: *Five* yuan.

Translation of the substitutes

①*pear, one*   ②*watermelon, five*   ③*banana, two*
④*pineapple, ten*

Supplementary words:

桃	táo	peach
葡萄	pútao	grape
草莓	cǎoméi	strawberry
杏	xìng	apricot
樱桃	yīngtao	cherry
枣	zǎo	date

Reference game 1

Invite a student to stand in front with his back towards the class. Put a new word card on the student's back. The student tries to guess the word with hints from the teacher. The student has three chances, if he is unable to guess correctly after the third try, let other students give the answer. If the student gives the correct answer, award him a colored sticker.

Reference game 2

This is a game of words of foods or fruits from the previous lessons. Divide the students into groups of two. One student says a word and the other student says another with the first letter initiated by the last letter of the previous one. The student saying the most words will be the winner.

Grammar:

(1) 一斤苹果<u>多少</u>钱？ (How much is a kilo of apples?)

"多少" is an interrogative pronoun for asking numbers or prices. It is generally used in asking numbers above ten, and "多少钱？" may be used for asking price as well.

For example: 你们班有多少个学生？ (How many students are there in your class?)

一个汉堡包多少钱？ (How much is a hamburger?)

"斤" is a weight measure word, and 1斤＝500g.

(2) 五<u>元</u>。

"元" is a measure word and a basic monetary unit for Chinese yuan or Renmenbi (RMB). In spoken Chinese "块" is also used.

▲▼ 2. Can you try?

Steps: (1) Put all the vocabulary cards about fruits on the board and mark the prices below each card.

(2) Ask a student to invite a classmate to do a question-and-answer exercise, e.g., A asks "一斤西瓜多少钱？" and B answers "五元"；A continues to ask "两斤西瓜多少钱？" and B should answer immediately. A tries to ask more difficult questions to stump B, like "一斤西瓜和三斤香蕉多少钱？"

(3) Student B questions A in the same way. The game continues until one student makes a mistake or gives the wrong answer.

(4) The most accurate student will get a colored sticker.

◆ 3. Let's talk. (CD)

Steps: (1) Ask students to listen to the CD, and then read aloud in different roles and do a role-play.

(2) Students perform in groups and award the best one.

Translation script:

Shop assistant: Hello! What can I do for you?

Fangfang: I like to buy apples and pears. How much is half-kilo of apples?

Shop assistant: Four yuan.

Fangfang: How much is half-kilo of pears?

Shop assistant: Three yuan.

Fangfang: I want to buy half-kilo of apples and half-kilo of pears.

Shop assistant: Seven yuan.

▲▼ 4. Do you know? (CD-ROM)

Abacus—An Ancient Calculator

The Abacus is the oldest calculator invented by the Chinese. The ancient Chinese calculated with small wooden sticks called "筹算" (to calculate with chips). Later with the development and increase of the production of grain and livestock, the small wooden sticks were inadequate and people began to use beads of different colors for calculation.

However using loose beads was cumbersome and inconvenient as the beads always rolled around. Therefore the Chinese began to string the beads on wooden sticks and fix them in a wooden frame. That was the origin of the abacus. Making an abacus is simple and costs little, and it is very versatile for calculating as well. The abacus is also easy to carry around as it need no power source thus saving energy.

Using abacus requires a good coordination of brain, eyes and hands, and is very effective in exercising and training the mind. Experts using the simple abacus can even rival the calculating speed of a modern calculator!

▲▼ 5. Learn to read. (CD, CD-ROM)

A Tongue Twister
Eating grapes without spitting peels,
While spitting peels without eating grapes.

▲▼ 6. Learn to write. (CD-ROM)

果

"果" in inscriptions on bones or tortoise shells resembles a fruit tree bearing much fruit. With its original meaning of "fruits on trees" "果" later expanded its meaning as "result" or "outcome of something" e.g., 结果(result or outcome).

Passing on messages game: Students in groups pass a brief verbal message to each other and find out the most accurate and fastest group.

Steps: (1) Divide the students into two rows with 6 to 10 students each.

(2) Prepare in advance written brief messages with four group of words or phrases e.g., 梨,苹果,香蕉,西瓜 or一斤苹果二斤西瓜，三斤香蕉 and 四斤梨.

(3) Show the message to the last student of each row. The student then whispers the message to the student in front of him or her one by one till the message reaches the first student in the row. Students are not allowed to discuss or speak aloud during the game.

(4) Upon receiving the message, the student at the front of each row tells the message or checks out the message on the vocabulary cards, and puts the words or phrases in correct order on the board.

(5) The group that finishes it first with accuracy will be rewarded.

⬩ **8. Story time.** (CD, CD-ROM)

① How much is a watermelon?
   Six yuan.
② A watermelon, please.

③ An apple, please.

④ A peach, please.

⑤ Here is a peach for you.

⑥ Oh? Where is the fruit?

▲▼ 1. Add the missing parts to the characters.

Steps: (1) Students look at the pictures, and then read the Chinese characters on the fruit.

(2) Ask students to find the missing radicals or strokes of the Chinese characters and complete them.

▲▼ 2. Write the tone mark for each *pinyin* and draw.

Steps: (1) Students read the *pinyin* and mark the tones.

(2) Guess the meaning of the *pinyin* words according to the tones.

(3) Draw corresponding objects according to the meaning of the words.

▲▼ 3. Count the numbers.

Steps: Students look at the pictures. Count the number of each food and fill in the blanks with the *pinyin* or Chinese characters.

Answers:

liù	sān	wǔ	jiǔ	shí	sì
六	三	五	九	十	四

▲ 4. Listen, match and say. (CD)

Steps: (1) Ask students to say the new words according to the pictures.

(2) Students listen to the CD and match each picture to its correct price.

(3) Correct them when necessary and give the answers.

Answers:

Shūbāo èrshíbā yuán. Bǐ shíqī yuán.
①书包 二十八 元。 笔 十七 元。

Màozi shí'èr yuán. Wàzi bā yuán.
②帽子 十二 元。 袜子 八 元。

Máoyī liùshí yuán. Hànbǎobāo shí yuán.
③毛衣 六十 元。 汉堡包 十 元。

Bīngqílín yì yuán. Xiāngjiāo wǔ yuán. Xīguā sān yuán.
④冰淇淋 一 元。 香蕉 五 元。 西瓜 三 元。

▲ 5. Listen and stick. (CD)

Steps: (1) Student read the English and try to understand the question.

(2) Student listen to the CD. Then choose the correct colored stickers in sticker pages and put them on the "big bag".

CD script:

shū, bǐ, běnzi, píngguǒ hé lí.
书，笔，本子，苹果 和 梨。

▲ 6. Fill in the blanks.

Steps: (1) Students understand the meaning of the four pictures.

(2) Students read the dialogue. Then fill in the missing parts.

(3) The teacher asks questions and then gives the correct answers.

(4) Students practise the dialogue in different roles.

Answers:

Shop assistant:
Nǐmen hǎo! Nǐmen mǎi shénme?
你们 好！ 你们 买 什么？

方方：
Yì jīn píngguǒ duōshao qián?
一 斤 苹果 多少 钱？

Shop assistant:
Wǔ yuán
五 元。

妈妈：
Yì jīn xiāngjiāo duōshao qián?
一 斤 香蕉 多少 钱？

Shop assistant:
Sān yuán.
三 元。

妈妈：
Wǒ mǎi yì jīn píngguǒ hé èr jīn
我 买 一 斤 苹果 和 二 斤
xiāngjiāo.
香蕉。

Shop assistant:
Shíyī yuán.
十一 元。

7. Look and say.

Steps: (1) Ask students to look at the picture for one minute and try to remember as many words as possible including the words hidden in corners.

(2) Students close their book. The teacher then asks the students to recall the words. Award the student who says the most words according to the picture a colored sticker.

8. How many things can you buy?

Steps: (1) Students read the name and price of each article.

(2) Then use 50 yuan to buy as many articles as possible or

without a cash surplus.

(3) Finally write the names and the prices of the articles in the form. Then add up.

HOMEWORK

Get students to think and design the looks of computers of the future by using their imagination and the cultural knowledge of this lesson.

UNIT FOUR DAILY LIFE

Lesson 7

I HAVE CHINESE TODAY.

Focus: School Life

Objective: Patterns: 你今天有什么课？

我今天没有课。

Vocabulary: 数学，历史，英语，汉语，

体育，地理，课，没有

Chinese Characters: 体，育

Culture: Class Schedule of China's Pupils

Teaching aids: (1) a class schedule

(2) a self-made dice with each surface written

with a subject to be learned in this lesson

(3) a pair of scissors, glue, cardboard and

crayons

(4) five cards for each subject

Review and introduction

(1) Check homework: invite students to show their drawings of computers of the future and talk about the ideas in their designs.

(2) Ask students in English what subjects they have for the day's class. Then write on the board the students' answers as an introduction to the new lesson.

◆ 1. Can you say? (CD)

Translation of the dialogue

What classes do you have today?

I have *Chinese* today.

I have no class today.

Translation of the substitutes

①*maths* ②*PE* ③*history* ④*English* ⑤*geography*

Supplementary words:

生物	shēngwù	biology
自然	zìrán	nature
手工	shǒugōng	handwork

Grammar:

(1) 我<u>今天</u>有汉语课。(I have Chinese today.)

A word or phrase restricting or modifying a predicate is called an adverbial adjunct. An adverbial adjunct always precedes the head word restricted or modified. In this sentence"今天" is an

adverbial adjunct to express time, which can be put either before or after the subject.

> For example: 昨天她去商店了。(Yesterday she went to the shop.)
>
> 我明天有数学课。(I have maths tomorrow.)

(2) 我今天<u>没有</u>课。(I have no class today.)

"没有" is a negative form of verb "有". Here it is a negation to possession or ownership.

> For example: 我没有汉语书。(I have no Chinese book.)
>
> 房间里没有电视。(There is no television in the room.)

▲▼ 2. Can you try?

Design a class schedule

Steps: (1) Draw an enlarged class schedule on the board and prepare some subject cards which can be stuck on the board.

(2) Make a big dice with the students (write the six subjects of this lesson on the surface of the dice).

(3) Ask "你们星期一有什么课？" and ask the students to take turns to throw the dice. The teacher or a student sticks the subject card to the class schedule on the board according to the result of each throw.

(4) In this way a student-designed class schedule is made according to the subjects from Monday to Friday.

(5) Then ask the class in English: "Do you like the class schedule you have designed?" If the answer is negative, the teacher can lead the class to design again or restore the class schedule to its original form.

3. Let's talk. (CD)

Steps: (1) Characters introduction: Xiaolong and Annie. They are at the school gate.

(2) Listen to the CD. Then the teacher reads aloud. Students follow and imitate.

(3) The teacher explains and translates the dialogue. Then students do role play performance.

Translation script:

Xiaolong: Do you have PE class today?

Annie: No.

Xiaolong: What classes do you have today?

Fangfang: Chinese, history and music.

Xiaolong: What classes do you have tomorrow?

Fangfang: It will be Saturday tomorrow, and we have no classes.

4. Do you know? (CD-ROM)

Class Schedule of Chinese Pupils

Formal education for Chinese children begins in the elementary school (at the age of seven). The subject courses of Chinese pupils are wide and varied. These subjects include maths, Chinese, English, history, geography, nature, politics, music, PE and arts. School life for lower grade children are relaxing and happy, however, when they reach the fifth or sixth grade, their happy childhood becomes fond memories. In order to prepare the students for a good and reputable middle school, courses such as arts and PE are gradually reduced. Students become busier and feel greater pressure with their studies than before.

▲▼ 5. Learn to read. (CD, CD-ROM)

A Proverb:

If you put in a lot of work, you can grind an iron rod into a needle.

▲▼ 6. Learn to write. (CD-ROM)

▲▼ 7. Let's do it. (CD-ROM)

Make a Three-dimensional Class Schedule

Steps: (1) Prepare a piece of rectangular cardboard. Fold it into four equal shares and paste it into a triangle prism.

(2) Along one of the three sidelines cut two slits: one at the upper part and the other at the lower part.

(3) Make a class schedule at the place between the two slits and draw beautiful pictures around it.

(4) Stick a photograph or a small picture.

▲▼ 8. Let's sing. (CD, CD-ROM)

So Many Cattle

So many cattle, so many cattle, the cattle dot the slope.
They are eating fresh grass, and
they are listening to pastoral songs.

WORKBOOK

◆ 1. Write and classify.

Steps: (1) Students read. Then learn to write the Chinese characters in the frames below according to the given order of the strokes.

(2) Find the stickers about "体育". Then put them in the six circles.

◆ 2.Match them and write.

Steps: 1. Students read aloud the Chinese characters on each of the book.

2. Then match them into words.

3. Finally write the matched words on the lines below.

Answers:
　　　yīnyuè　　Hànyǔ　　tǐyù　　dìlǐ　　lìshǐ　　shùxué
　　①音乐　②汉语　③体育　④地理　⑤历史　⑥数学

◆ 3. Color them and write.

Steps: (1) Students find the relevant air bubbles for the colorful fish. Then color the bubbles with the same color as that of the fish.

(2) Students write the *pinyin* in the blanks below the fish according to the meanings of the words inside the air bubbles.

Answers:
　　　　　　tǐyù　　　　　lǐshǐ　　　　　Hànyǔ
　　PE→体育；history→历史；Chinese→汉语
　　　　　　shùxué　　　　yīnyuè　　　　Yīngyǔ
　　maths→数学；music→音乐；English→英语

geography→地理
dìlǐ

◆ 4. Find and say.

Steps: (1) Invite students to think about the corresponding class wherever a picture is seen from "start".

(2) Students say loudly the class names and the teacher corrects when necessary.

Answer:

yīnyuè kè   tǐyù   kè   Yīngyǔ kè   lìshǐ   kè
音乐 课→体育 课→英语 课→历史 课→

shùxué kè   Hànyǔ kè   dìlǐ   kè
数学 课→汉语 课→地理 课

◆ 5. Listen and fill in the blanks. (CD)

Step: Students look at the pictures. Then listen to the CD and fill in blanks with correct class names.

CD script:

Bā diǎn yǒu shùxué kè   jiǔ diǎn yǒu Yīngyǔ kè,
星期一：8 点 有 数学 课，9 点 有 英语 课，

shí diǎn yǒu lìshǐ   kè,   shíyī diǎn yǒu tǐyù   kè.
10 点 有 历史 课，11 点 有 体育 课。

Bā diǎn yǒu Hànyǔ kè   jiǔ diǎn yǒu yīnyuè kè,
星期二：8 点 有 汉语 课，9 点 有 音乐 课，

shí diǎn yǒu shùxué kè,   shíyī diǎn yǒu dìlǐ   kè.
10 点 有 数学 课，11 点 有 地理 课。

◆ 6. Look and answer.

Step: Ask students to look at the class schedule, and then answer the questions one by one.

Answers :

① Méiyǒu.
没有。

② Yǒu.
有。

③ Yǒu Yīngyǔ kè, shùxué kè　Hànyǔ kè hé
有 英语 课、数学 课、汉语 课 和
tǐyù　kè.
体育 课。

④ Méiyǒu.
没有。

⑤ Méiyǒu kè.
没有 课。

◆ 7. Do a report.

Steps: (1) Students read the subject name on each textbook.

(2) Students add the numbers of each subject in a week and draw stars as substitution for the numbers at the back of each textbook.

(3) Students find out which subject has the most classes.

HOMEWORK

By way of learning through play, students learn new words by means of self-designing and at the same time develop their interest and creativity this way.

UNIT FOUR DAILY LIFE

Lesson 8

I AM GOING ON THE INTERNET.

Focus: Daily Life

Objective: Patterns:你在做什么？

我在上网。

Vocabulary:上网，睡觉，吃饭，洗澡，报
纸，作业，写，在，做

Chinese Characters: 洗，澡

Culture: Life of Chinese Pupils after Class

Teaching aids: (1) a self-made clock

(2) props (cards or head ornaments) about
the animals learned previously

(3) figure cards such as father, mother,
Fangfang and vocabulary verb cards learned
before such as 看，写，吃，做，玩

STUDENT'S BOOK

Review and introduction

(1) Ask students to show their designs——textbook covers and explain their ideas. Then choose excellent designs and stick them to the board.

(2) Pick up a student's stationery randomly and ask the price as a review of the previous lesson.

(3) Take out a clock, set it to the present time and ask the class: "现在几点？" Then in English: "What are you doing now?" Students answer: "We're having class." as an introduction to the new lesson.

1. Can you say? (CD)

Translation of the dialogue

What are *you* doing?

I am *going on the Internet*.

Translation of the substitutes

① have dinner

② read newspaper

③ sleep

④ have a shower

⑤ do homework

Supplementary words:

洗脸	xǐ liǎn	wash one's face
刷牙	shuā yá	brush one's teeth
打电话	dǎ diànhuà	make a call
做饭	zuò fàn	cook

A game

There are some verb-object phrases to learn in this lesson so the emphasis of this game should be practising how to arrange verb-object phrases.

Steps: (1) Take out the prepared vocabulary cards such as "看", "写", "吃", "做", "玩", "打" and stick them randomly on the board.

(2) Have students think about the objects which can collocate with these verbs.

(3) Invite a student to come to the front and pick up a card he or she knows and then says aloud the relevant verb-object phrase.

(4) Writes the correct answers on the board and lead the students to read along to have a full understanding of the verb-object phrases.

Grammar

我在上网。(I am going on the Internet.)

"在" is an adverb which can be put before a predicate to indicate that an action is in progress. The action may take place either in the present, the past or the future. Both "正在" and "正" indicate that an action is in progress. "呢" can be put at the end of a sentence with "在", "正" or "正在" to form the construction "在……呢" or "正在……呢".

For example: 我在写作业。(I am doing homework.)

小王在唱歌呢。(Xiaowang is singing.)

他正在吃饭呢。(He is having s meal.)

◆ 2. Can you try?

Steps: (1) Divide the class into groups of four to act as a family. One student dresses up as an aide with a clock to give the time. The other three students dress up as father, mother and child.

(2) The play includes: the aide choosing three points in time——morning, noon and aftcrnoon and pointing at the time when each family member is doing something different. For example, the aide sets the clock to six o'clock and asks the class "现在几点？" and the class gives the answer.

(3) The aide then asks: "爸爸在做什么？" and the father answers with the action: "爸爸在看电视。" The aside continues to ask : "妈妈在做什么?" and "你在做什么?" The mother and child respond with appropriate actions.

◆ 3. Let's talk. (CD)

Steps: (1) Characters introduction: Jack and Mum. Translate and explain the dialogue.

(2) Students listen to the CD and then read aloud in different roles and do the role play in groups.

Translation:

Mum: What's the time?

Jack: 9 o'clock in the evening.

Mum: What's your younger brother doing?

Jack: He's taking a bath.

Mum: How about your elder brother and elder sister?

Jack: They are doing their homework.

4. Do you know? (CD-ROM)

Life of Chinese Pupils after Class

The school life of Chinese pupils is rather busy but their activities after school are wide and varied. In the afternoon they usually have private tutoring classes such as calligraphy, music, foreign languages, physical exercises, and Chinese chess etc. after class. They also enjoy watching Television shows or cartoons, surfing the Internet and playing electronic computer games etc..

In spring and autumn large-scale sports meetings, singing or poem reciting competitions, and special outings are held. Students yearn and look forward to all these activities eagerly.

5. Learn to read. (CD, CD-ROM)

An Ancient Poem

Reflections on a Quiet Night

Before my bed shine bright the silver beams,

It seems the autumn frost on the ground so gleams.

I gaze upwards toward the moon in the skies,

And downwards look when a nostalgia does arise.

▲▼ 6. Learn to write. (CD-ROM)

氵 （水）

The radical " 氵 "is developed from the Chinese character "水" (see the explanation in Lesson 11 STUDENT'S BOOK 1B). Therefore the meanings of Chinese characters with the radical " 氵 " are all related to "水", e.g., "江 （river） , 河 （river） ,湖 （lake） ,海 （sea） ,汁 （juice） and 泪 （tear） ".

▲▼ 7. Let's do it. (CD-ROM)

Idiom story performance: The Fox Assuming the Majesty of the Tiger

Steps: (1) Introduce the story according to the pictures.

(2) Have students prepare the props and act either in Chinese or in English according to their language proficiency.

(3) Assign the roles and conduct rehearsals.

(4) The class may perform in public. The teacher appraises the excellent.

The story:

The Chinese like to express their ideas by using set phrases composed of four characters. Many idioms are related to stories about animals. Today let us introduce an idiom related to "虎".

The Fox Assuming the Majesty of the Tiger

One day a tiger captured a fox in the forest. When it was about to eat the fox, the fox said: "How dare you eat me? I am appointed by God to govern all the beasts. If you eat me, you will make God angry." The tiger did not believe the fox, but the fox added: "if you don't believe me, you may follow me to see how the other beasts run away when they see me." The tiger hesitated and decided to go along with the fox. As they went on their way, all the other beasts ran away at the sight of them. On seeing this, the tiger thought that the other beasts were afraid of the fox, not realizing whom they were really afraid of! Thus the tiger believed the fox and did not eat him!

"狐假虎威" originated from this story. Now, it is used to refer to those who take advantage of someone else's power to bully others.

▲▼ 8. Story time. (CD, CD-ROM)

① What shall I do?

② Hello, I'm the teacher of the little rabbit. Tomorrow we'll have a maths test.

③ Thanks a lot.

④ Go home! Tomorrow you'll have a maths test.

⑤ Today we'll have a test.

WORKBOOK

▲▼ 1. Stick and write.

Steps: (1) Students read the *pinyin* and guess the meaning of the two characters.

(2) Students find out the missing stroke stickers from the sticker pages. Then put them in the frames to complete the two characters.

(3) Students practise the Chinese characters and count the number of strokes for each character.

2. Find and color them.

Steps: (1) Students look at the pictures. Then find out the correct collocation of each phrase.

(2) Students color each phrase.

Answers: shuìjiào / xǐzǎo /shàng wǎng / kàn bàozhǐ /xiě zuòyè

睡觉／ 洗澡／上 网／ 看 报纸／写 作业

3. Match them and say.

Steps: (1) Students look at the clock to know the time.

(2) Students match the pictures with the phrases. Then color the phrases with their favorite colors.

Answers:

shàng wǎng　　　kàn bàozhǐ

① 上 网　② 看 报纸

xiě zuòyè　　　shuìjiào

③ 写 作业　④ 睡觉

4. What does Mingming usually do after noon?

Step: Students write down the actions according to the timetable.

Answers:

Míngming zài xué Hànyǔ.

①明明　 在 学 汉语。

Míngming zài shàng wǎng.

②明明　 在 上 网。

Míngming zài xiě zuòyè.

③明明　 在 写 作业。

Míngming   zài chī fàn.

④明明　 在 吃 饭。

Míngming zài kàn diànshì.

⑤明明　 在 看 电视。

Míngming   zài   xǐzǎo.
⑥ 明明   在 洗澡。

Míngming   zài   shuìjiào.
⑦ 明明   在 睡觉。

♦ 5. Listen, choose and color them. (CD)

Steps: (1) Students listen to the CD. Then choose the answers.

(2) Students color the dotted pictures according to the

answers.

CD script:

Xiànzài wǔ diǎn, Nánxī zài xiě zuòyè.
①现在 五 点，南希 在 写 作业。

Xiànzài qī diǎn,   Ānni zài xǐzǎo.
②现在 七 点，安妮 在 洗澡。

Xiànzài xiàwǔ sān diǎn, Jiékè zài dǎ pīngpāngqiú.
③现在 下午 三 点，杰克 在 打 乒乓球。

Xiànzài wǎnshang bā diǎn, Fāngfang zài kàn bàozhǐ.
④现在 晚上 八 点，方方 在 看 报纸。

Answers: ①B ②C ③A ④A

♦ 6. Look, say and act it out.

Steps: (1) Students look at the pictures. Then say one by one

what the animals are doing.

(2) Students do the role play with the animal props.

Answers:

Xióngmāo zài chī fàn.
①熊猫   在 吃 饭。

Mǎ zài hē shuǐ.
②马 在 喝 水。

Tùzi   zài xǐzǎo.
③兔子 在 洗澡。

Māo zài shuìjiào.
④猫   在 睡觉。

Xiǎoniǎo zài chàng gēr.
⑤小鸟 在 唱 歌儿。

Jīnyú zài yóuyǒng.
⑥金鱼 在 游泳。

⬦ 7. Interview your classmates.

Steps: (1) Students look at the pictures and read the questions.
Then interview your classmates.

(2) Students write three answers for each question.

HOMEWORK

Have students draw activity pictures of their own family members at a particular time. Then tell the class.

UNIT FIVE TRAFFIC & TRAVEL

Lesson 9

HOW TO GET TO THE BOOKSTORE?

Focus: Traffic

Objective: Patterns: 请问，书店怎么走？

往左走。

Vocabularys: 前，后，左，右，书店，请问，

怎么，往，走

Chinese Character: 左，右

Culture: China's Traffic

Teaching aids: (1) traffic sign cards: red light, green light,

stop and go

(2) a scarf for hide-and-seek

STUDENT'S BOOK

Review and introduction

(1) Check homework and review the last lesson. Invite each student to tell the class what his family members are doing at a particular time.

(2) Dresse up as a passerby or a traveler and ask the students: "Excuse me, how do I get to the bookstore?" Then draw direction indicators on the board and ask the class to tell the directions as an introduction to the new lesson.

1. Can you say? (CD)

Explain according to the pictures of the text while writing the direction signs "前", "后", "左" and "右" on the board. Then lead students to mark the symbolic buildings such as bookstore, school, hospital, supermarket and park on the board. Finally, ask the class with the sentence patterns of this text and let the students give the directions.

Translation of the dialogue

Excuse me, how do I get to the *bookstore*?
Turn to the *left*.

Translation of the substitutes

① *park*   ② *school*   ③ *station*
④ *forward*   ⑤ *left*   ⑥ *right*

Supplementary words:

东	dōng	east
西	xī	west
南	nán	south
北	běi	north
警察	jǐngchá	policeman

Grammar:

(1) 请问，书店怎么走？(Excuse me, how do I get to the bookstore?)

"请问" is a polite expression often placed at the beginning of a sentence for inquiry.

For example: 请问，超市怎么走？(Excuse me, how do I get to the supermarket?)

请问，你会汉语吗？(Excuse me, can you speak Chinese?)

"怎么" is a demonstrative pronoun. "怎么＋动词" is used for inquiring the way of an action.

For example: 这个字怎么写？(How is this character written?)

你怎么来的？(How did you come?)

(2) 往左走。

"往" is a preposition indicating direction. It can be put before a location noun or a noun phrase to form a prepositional phrase which usually precedes a verb.

For example: 往右看。(Look toward right.)

往前走。(Go forward.)

▲▼ 2. Can you try?

Steps: (1) Lead the class to the schoolyard. Then draw a big

74

direction indicator on the ground and mark "前", "后", "左" and "右" on it.

(2) Stick the vocabulary cards of places (such as school, hospital, shop) learned in previous lessons to the backs of some students .

(3) Arrange the students with the vocabulary cards to stand at certain points on the direction indicator.

(4) Ask the other students: "××怎么走?" and the students answer in chorus: "往×走" according to the position of the student with that particular card.

3. Let's talk. (CD)

Steps: (1) Characters introduction: the policeman, Annie and sister. Then translate and explain the dialogue.

(2) Students listen to the CD, then read aloud in different roles and do a role play.

(3) Students perform in groups and reward the best group.

Translation script:

> Annie: Look! " Stop when the red light is on, and walk when the green light is on."
>
> Annie: Excuse me, how do I get to the station?
>
> Policeman: Turn to the right.
>
> Annie: Thank you!

4. Do you know? (CD-ROM)

China's Traffic

In China there are many different modes of transportation such as bus, subway, tramcar, taxi, car and bicycle etc. As China is a vast country with a large population, bicycle is still the most important means of transport for the majority of the people. Almost every Chinese family has a bicycle, therefore during rush hours some city's main streets become a sea of bicycles. With the rising living standards more and more families own cars. China's traffic regulations require the use of the right side of the road for traffic movements. At the crossroads not only are there traffic lights installed but there are also traffic policemen keeping the order and providing assistance for those in need.

▲▼ 5. Learn to read. (CD, CD-ROM)

A Tongue Twister
There are traffic lights at the crossroad,
Please tell green, yellow and red.
Green and red, red and green.
Seeing the lights, then go and stop, stop and go.

▲▼ 6. Learn to write. (CD-ROM)

▲▼ 7. Let's do it. (CD-ROM)

Hide-and-seek: stop as red light's on and go as green light's on
Steps: (1) Lead the class outdoors and draw or mark a 10m² square.

(2) All the students stand in the square. Choose a student (using "stone, scissors and cloth" game) and blindfold the student.

(3) When the blindfolded student gives the order "绿灯行", the other students begin walking freely within the square. When "红灯停" is given, all students stop at once and remain motionless. Any student who moves will be treated as having broken the rules and will be

penalized.

(4) When the blindfolded student captures a student,he is supposed to guess the student's name by touching. If he or she guesses right, the captured student will be blindfolded to continue the game.

8. Let's sing. (CD, CD-ROM)

Go Traveling

Stop at the red light, and go on at the green.

In my car, I go traveling.

By ship, by plane,

I go to Shanghai and Beijing.

Turn left and turn right,

I have good friends everywhere.

"Excuse me."

"Thank you."

"You are welcome."

I have good friends everywhere.

WORKBOOK

1. Add the missing parts to the characters.

Steps: (1) Students guess the meaning of the Chinese characters according to the English.

(2) Students complete the Chinese characters by adding their missing parts.

2. Say as quickly as you can.

Steps: (1) Students read the direction indicators "前"，"后"，

"左", "右" and learn them by heart.

(2) From the entrance students say the direction of each arrow as quickly as they can.

▲ 3. Listen and stick. (CD)

Steps: (1) Students look at the picture. Then open the sticker pages.

(2) Students listen to the CD.

(3) Students choose the correct stickers according to the CD. Then put them up.

CD script: Yóujú wǎng qián zǒu, túshūguǎn wǎng zuǒ zǒu, xuéxiào
邮局 往 前 走，图书馆 往 左 走，学校
wǎng yòu zǒu, shāngdiàn wǎng yòu zǒu,
往 右 走，商店 往 右 走，
gōngyuán wǎng qián zǒu.
公园 往 前 走。

▲ 4. Find the way.

Steps: (1) Students read the given part of the dialogue. Then walk from the entrance with a finger or a pen to find the bookstore.

(2) Then fill in the blank.

Answer: Wǎng yòu zǒu.
往 右 走。

▲ 5. Color them and choose.

Steps: (1) Ask Students to look at the pictures and decide whether the traffic light should be red or green.

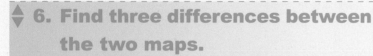

(2) Students color the traffic lights and fill the right selections in the blanks below the pictures.

Answers: ①B　②A

6. Find three differences between the two maps.

step: Students look at the pictures and find out the three differences.

Answers: ①红绿灯　②警察手势　③指向标

7. Answer the questions.

Steps: (1) Students look at the picture and locate the buildings according to the signs on the picture.

(2) Students read the questions and answer according to the picture.

Answers:

         Wǎng qián zǒu.
① 往　前　走。

         Wǎng qián zǒu.
② 往　前　走。

         Wǎng zuǒ zǒu.
③ 往　左　走。

         Wǎng yòu zǒu.
④ 往　右　走。

HOME WORK

Ask Students to interview some classmates and complete a form of directions to get to different places from school.

UNIT FIVE **TRAFFIC & TRAVEL**

Lesson 10

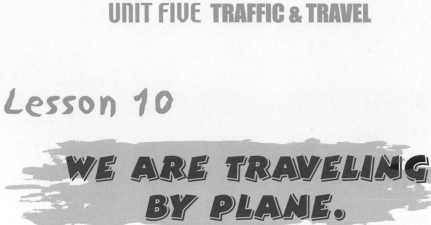

WE ARE TRAVELING BY PLANE.

Focus: Travel

Objective: Patterns:我们坐飞机去旅行。

Vocabulary: 飞机，火车，汽车，轮船，自行车，坐，骑，旅行

Chinese Characters: 火，车

Culture: China's Main Tourist Cities

Teaching aids: (1) a trourist map of China, pictures of scenic spots and historical sites such as Tian An Men, Terra-cotta Warriors and Horses etc.

(2) vehicle models

(3) crayons, a cardboard and paper clips

STUDENT'S BOOK

Review and introduction

    (1) Check students' homework: invite some students to say how to get to a bookstore, hospital, post office, shop, park and supermarket from school as a review of the words and patterns of last lesson.

    (2) Ask students in English: "Do you like traveling?", and "what places have you been to?" Then write down the names of these places and ask: "How did you get there?" Students give answers such as "by plane", "by train", "by boat etc." Finally introduce the new lesson "坐飞机去旅行。"

▲ 1. Can you say? (CD)

    Take out the city pictures (learned previously) and stick them on the board and say "这是上海","这是北京","我们在北京，我们坐飞机去上海" while pointing to the direction of Beijing with the plane model. Then choose other places and lead students to practise with the models of train, car, boat etc..

Translation of the dialogue

We are traveling *by plane*.

Translation of the substitutes

①*by train* ②*by ship* ③*by car* ④*by bike*

Supplementary words:

出租车	chūzūchē	taxi
摩托车	mōtuōchē	motorbike
开	kāi	drive

Grammar:

我们坐飞机去旅行。(We are traveling by plane.)

A sentence in which two or more verbs or verbal constructions are taken as the predicate is called a sentence with verbal constructions in series. The relations between the two verbs are varied. The relation which is introduced in this lesson is one in which the first verb or verb construction indicates the means or manner of the following action.

For example: 他们坐汽车去学校。(They go to school by bus.)

我坐飞机去(上海)。(I travel (to Shanghai) by plane.)

◆ 2. Can you try?

Steps: (1) Lead students outdoors.

(2) Choose students' favorite tourist destinations and put the corresponding vocabulary cards or pictures by the wooden sticks. Then place the wooden sticks in different locations.

(3) Divide the class into groups of five. Ask each group to stay close in a row without wandering away or splitting up.

(4) Read a sentence loudly, for example, "坐飞机去上海。" and ask students to simulate the type and sound of the vehicle and run to the destination. See which group

gets to the destination first.

(5) The group which reaches the destination first and in good order will be rewarded with colored stickers.

◆ 3. Let's talk. (CD)

Steps: (1) Students listen to the CD, read aloud in different roles and do imitation and substitution practices.

(2) Ask students to perform in groups and reward the best group.

Translation:

Jack: I want to go traveling.

Annie: Where will you go?

Jack: Beijing and Hongkong.

Annie: How will you get there?

Jack: I will get there by train.

◆ 4. Do you know? (CD-ROM)

China's Major Tourist Cities

China is rich in tourist resources. Historical sites and natural scenic spots are spread all over the country. Here is a very brief introduction of some famous Chinese tourist cities.

Beijing is both an ancient cultural city and China's political, economic and cultural center. There are many scenic spots and historical sites which belong to the world cultural heritages, such as the Great Wall, the Forbidden City, the Summer Palace, the Temple of Heaven, the site of the Ruins of Yuanmingyuan and the Ming Tombs.

Shanghai is a well developed modern city with famous

scenic spots such as the Bund and the Oriental TV Tower.

Harbin is a famous northern tourist city. It is cool in summer and in winter it is famous for its ice and snow activities, festivals of ice lantern and sculptors.

Xi'an, the ancient capital of six dynasties, is one of the oldest cities in China. Historical sites and scenic spots such as the Terra-cotta Warriors and Horses, the Huaqing Pool, the Big Wildgoose Pagoda and Mount Hua are all located here.

Hong Kong, one of the special administrative regions of China, is a center of world finance, trade and business. It is also famous for shopping and tourism.

Suzhou and Hangzhou which are abundant in silk and tea are both famous cities in the south of the Yangtze River. They are also world famous for their gardens and specialties of rivers and lakes.

♦ 5. Learn to read. (CD, CD-ROM)

An Ancient Poem

On the Stork Tower

Along the mountains sink the last rays of sun,

Towards the sea the Yellow River does forward go.

If you would fain command a thousand miles in view,

To a higher storey you are expected to go.

♦ 6. Learn to write. (CD-ROM)

火

Its original meaning is fire. In inscriptions on bones or tortoise shells, "火" resembles a fire that is burning. Chinese characters with "火" as its radical have meanings related to fire, such as "灯"(lamp or light), "烧"(burn) etc..

车

In inscription on bones or tortoise shells, "车" resembles the shape of a carriage. Chinese characters with "车" as its radical have meanings related to vehicle, such as "轮(wheel)，转(revolve)，军(troops)" etc..

7. Let's do it. (CD-ROM)

Paper Folding: Make a Paper Plane

Steps: (1) Have each student prepare two pieces of colored paper.

(2) Practise to fold a paper plane: one is folded according to the traditional method, and the other is folded according to a new method. Example pictures follow.

(3) Lead students outdoors to have a flying match to see which plane can fly higher and farther.

8. Story time. (CD, CD-ROM)

① We are going to the park!

② Excuse me, how do I get to the park? Turn left.

③ Excuse me, how do I get to the park? Turn left.

④ We want to go to the park, too!

⑤ Don't worry! Look, it's blowing!

⑥ We are going to the park by plane!

WORKBOOK

◆ 1. Write.

Steps: (1) Students look at the picture. Then trace the dotted Chinese characters.

(2) Students read the new words, and say their meanings.

◆ 2. Match them.

Steps: (1) Students look at the pictures in the first vertical row, then read the English.

(2) Students match them according to their meanings.

◆ 3. Draw and write.

Steps: (1) Students say the background of each picture under the teacher's instruction.

(2) The teacher asks what vehicles should be drawn on the different backgrounds.

(3) Students draw.

(4) Students fill the *pinyin* of each vehicle in the blanks.

◆ 4. Listen and stick.

Steps: (1) Ask students to open the sticker pages. Then find out the relevant stickers.

(2) Students listen to the CD and then put the correct stickers in the circle.

CD script:

Xiǎolóng zuò fēijī qù Měiguó.
① 小龙 坐 飞机 去 美国。

Fāngfang zuò lúnchuán qù Xiānggǎng.
② 方方 坐 轮船 去 香港。

Jiékè zuò huǒchē qù Shànghǎi.
③ 杰克 坐 火车 去 上海。

Gēge qí zìxíngchē qù xuéxiào.
④ 哥哥 骑 自行车 去 学校。

Ānni zuò qìchē qù shāngdiàn.
⑤ 安妮 坐 汽车 去 商店。

5. A race.

Steps: (1) Lead students to read aloud which vehicle each person uses to go to Hong Kong.

(2) Ask students to judge the order of arrival in Hong Kong using these four vehicles, and mark it.

6. Read and say.

Steps: (1) Students read aloud these place names.

(2) Ask students in Chinese "怎么去?"

(3) Students answer what vehicle they will choose and what place they will go.

7. Compose a dialogue.

Steps: (1) Ask students to look at the pictures and choose appropriate sentences to fill in the blanks.

(2) Divide the class into pairs and ask students to practise the dialogue according to the pictures.

Referential dialogue:

Xiǎolóng, nǐ hǎo!
Jack: 小龙， 你 好！

Nǐ hǎo!
小龙: 你 好！

Nǐ yào qù nǎr?
Jack: 你 要 去 哪儿？

Wǒ yào qù Xiānggǎng. Nǐ ne?
小龙: 我 要 去 香港。 你呢？

Wǒ qù Běijīng.
Jack: 我 去 北京。

Nǐ zěnme qù?
Jack: 你 怎么 去？

Wǒ zuò lúnchuán qù.
小龙: 我 坐 轮船 去。

Wǒ zuò huǒchē qù.
Jack: 我 坐 火车 去。

 **HOMEWORK**

A Drawing game:

Ask students to design a vehicle (a car or a plane) of the future and talk about its advantage to the class. By doing this it will help the students to exercise their imagination and ability to express themselves.

UNIT SIX BIRTHDAYS & FESTIVALS

Lesson 11

Focus: Birthday Congratulations

Objective: Patterns: 生日快乐!

爸爸送我一个礼物。

Vocabulary: 生日，蛋糕，礼物，手表，娃娃，

杯子，生日卡，快乐，送，个

Chinese Characters: 快，乐

Culture: The 12 Symbolic Animals Associated

with a 12-year Cycle

Teaching aids: (1) materials for making a birthday cap:

a cardboard, crayons, scissors, glue, etc.

(2) material objects: cup, doll, watch, etc.

(3) birthday cards

STUDENT'S BOOK

Review and introduction

(1) Check homework: let students show their drawings of the vehicle of the future and say in English the advantages of their designs.

(2) Assume that today is the birthday of student A. Take out a birthday card and say "生日快乐!" as an introduction to the topic of this lesson—— Birthday Congratulations.

◆ 1. Can you say? (CD)

Translation of the dialogue

It's my birthday today. *Daddy* gave me a *gift*.
Happy birthday!

Translation of the substitutes

①*mum, cake* ②*sister, cup* ③*brother, watch*
④*Annie, doll* ⑤*Jack, birthday card*

Supplementary words:

晚会	wǎnhuì	evening party
蜡烛	làzhú	candle
眼镜	yǎnjìng	glasses

Grammar:

(1) 爸爸送<u>我</u><u>一个</u>礼物。

This is a double objects sentence. In Chinese some transitive verbs can take two objects. The first, mostly a personal noun or pronoun, is an indirect object and the second, mostly a noun or phrase of non-personal reference, is the direct object. For example:

哥哥送我一个篮球。(Brother gave me a basketball.)

妈妈送我一个手表。(Mum gave me a watch.)

"个" is a measure word. It is generally placed before a noun which has no specific measure word, e.g., "一个人", "一个本子", "一个西瓜", "一个汉堡包"etc..

(2) 生日快乐！

This sentence is a short form for "祝你生日快乐"！It is used for congratulating on or blessing for one's birthday. Other similar congratulations:

新年快乐！（Happy New Year!）

春节快乐！（Happy Spring Festival!）

♦ 2. Can you try?

Steps: (1) Divide the class into groups of five. Suppose the student who dresses up as if today is his or her birthday is student A and the other students dress up as his or her friends.

(2) Student A writes his or her birth date on a card. The four friends draw their gifts on the other cards and prepare to go to the birthday party.

(3) The performance begins with student A holding a card saying "今天×月×日，是我的生日。" The four friends then come together and say "生日快乐。" Student A says "谢谢".

(4) The four friends give their gift cards one by one each saying "我送你一个××。"

(5) Student A shows the gifts and says "××送我一个××，××送我一个××。"

(6) Each group has 10 minutes for preparation. Comment and reward the best group after students' performance.

3. Let's talk (CD)

Steps: (1) Students listen to the CD, then imitate the dialogue in
different roles.

(2) Students come up to the front of the class to perform
in groups. Then the teacher comments and appraises.

Translation:

Annie: Today is my birthday.

Fangfang: Happy birthday.

A gift for you.

Annie: It's a doll!

It's very beautiful! Thanks!

4. Do you know? (CD-ROM)

The 12 Symbolic Animals Associated with a 12-year Cycle

The ancient Chinese used the ten Heavenly Stems combined with the twelve Earthly Branches to designate time. At the same time the ancient Chinese also used twelve kinds of animals as symbols of the twelve Earthly Branches to designate the birth year of a person. The twelve symbolic animals are: rat, ox, tiger, rabbit, dragon, snake, horse, sheep, monkey, rooster, dog, and pig. But why were these twelve animals chosen? Among the many stories about the choices of these animals here is an interesting one.

It was said that in ancient times there was no way to designate the time, so the Jade Emperor decided to hold a race and the first twelve animals to arrive will have their names on the twelve year cycle. At that time the cat and the rat were good friends. As both were afraid that they would oversleep on the day of the race, they asked the ox to wake them up early. In the morning of the race day the ox invited the cat and the rat to ride on his back to take part in the race. However, the rat pushed the sleeping cat into the water and jumped onto the riverbank when crossing the river and finished the race first. The ox came in second, the tiger was third and the rabbit fourth. The dragon, the fastest runner was fifth because he went to give rainfall in the east. Then came the snake, the horse, the sheep, the monkey, the rooster, the dog, and the pig who was the twelfth. The sleeping cat which was pushed into the water got nothing, therefore the cat and the rat became enemies forever. The twelve animals complete a cycle once every twelve years. Now you can calculate your own and your family members' symbolic animals according to the animal chart sign system in this text.

▲ 5. Learn to read. (CD, CD-ROM)

A Riddle
Although it seems aged,
And has lots of whiskers,
Anyone whomever it meets,
It will cry mummy.

▲ 6. Learn to write. (CD-ROM)

▲ 7. Let's do it. (CD-ROM)

Make a Colored Birthday Cap

Steps: (1) Prepare a cardboard, glue, crayons, etc..

(2) Roll a piece of square cardboard into a cone shape and wear it on the head to see whether it fits.

(3) Glue the paper cone. Then draw favorite pictures on it or stick colored ribbons to the edge of the cap. Thus a birthday cap is completed.

8. Let's sing. (CD, CD-ROM)

Happy Birthday

Happy birthday to you,

Happy birthday to you,

Happy birthday to you,

Happy birthday to you!

WORKBOOK

1. Write.

Steps: (1) Students read. Then trace the dotted lines of the characters in the frames according to the given order of the strokes.

(2) Students count the number of strokes of each character.

2. Listen and color them. (CD)

Steps: (1) Students look at the pictures. Then read the words represented by the pictures.

(2) Students listen to the CD. Then choose the correct pictures.

(3) Students color the picture they have chosen.

CD script:

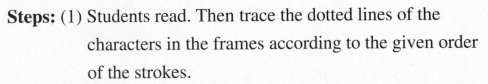

Bàba sòng wǒ yí ge shǒubiǎo.

① 爸爸 送 我 一个 手表。

Gēge sòng wǒ yí gè qiǎokèlì.
② 哥哥 送 我 一个 巧克力。

Jiějie sòng wǒ yí ge wáwa.
③ 姐姐 送 我 一个 娃娃。

Māma sòng wǒ yí ge shūbāo.
④ 妈妈 送 我 一个 书包。

3. Look and write.

Steps: (1) Students look at the pictures, then find the Chinese
characters which can be combined into phrases.

(2) Students write the new words on the lines.

Answers:

手表　杯子　蛋糕　生日　礼物　快乐

4. A maze.

Steps: (1) Students look for the right route to the exit from the
entrance.

(2) Students say the names of the gifts they have met on
the route. Check to see who does it best.

Answers:

dàngāo　shǒubiǎo　zìxíngchē
蛋糕　手表　自行车

5. Find out and say.

Steps: (1) Students look at the pictures, then find out the gifts
hidden in the picture and try to be the first to answer.

(2) The student who can answer the most will be rewarded.

Answers:

máoyī　xié　qiǎokèlì　shǒubiǎo　shǔpiànr　wáwa
毛衣　鞋　巧克力　手表　薯片儿　娃娃

bēizi   shū   bǐ   shēngrikǎ   dàngāo
杯子   书   笔   生日卡   蛋糕

6. Fill in the blanks.

Steps: (1) Students look at the picture and try to understand it.

(2) Students fill in the missing words according to the content of the paragraph.

Answers:

shí yuè wǔ rì   shēngri   dàngāo   shūbāo   wáwa
10 月 5 日   生日   蛋糕   书包   娃娃

shēngrikǎ   hǎokàn
生日卡   好看

7. Design birthday gifts for your family.

Steps: (1) Students write the birth dates of family members on the calendar.

(2) Then design a gift for each of them, and draw pictures of the gifts.

(3) Finally say what gifts you will give to your family members.

 HOMEWORK

Ask students to design a birthday card (giving free rein to their imagination) for a friend whose birthday is coming.

Lesson 12

THE NEW YEAR IS COMING.

Focus: Festivals

Objective: Patterns: 春节快到了！

Vocabulary: 春节，新年，圣诞节，爷爷，
奶奶，朋友，快，到

Chinese Characters: 朋，友

Culture: The Spring Festival

Teaching aids: (1) number cards, month and day cards, or a
calendar

(2) pictures about moon cakes, dumpling,
turkey and Santa Claus etc.

(3) a red paper envelope or packet

STUDENT'S BOOK

Review and introduction

(1) Ask students to take out the birthday cards designed for friends and give them to his or her classmates and say: 生日快乐。Or the teacher may ask if any student's birthday is coming and ask the class to sing a birthday song for that student.

(2) Take out the calendar, and turn to 1st, January. Then ask the class in English what festival 1st January is and write the answer "新年" on the board. Finally ask students to say "新年快乐!", then turn the calendar to 31st December to introduce the topic of this lesson——"新年快到了!"

1. Can you say? (CD)

Translation of the dialogue

A: The *New Year* is coming. What are you going to do?

B: I am going to *travel*.

Translation of the substitutes

① *Spring Festival, see my gramdpa and grandma.*

② *Christmas, see my friend*

Supplementary words:

感恩节	Gǎn'ēn Jié	Thanksgiving Day
中秋节	Zhōngqiū Jié	Mid-autumn Festival
儿童节	Értóng Jié	Children's Day

Grammar:

新年快到了！(The New Year is coming!)

"快" is an adverb indicating being close to a time or an imminent action taking place. "了" is usually put at the end of such sentence. "快……了" can have a verb, an adjective, a noun or a numeral measure word, etc. inserted between them. In this lesson it is "快＋verb＋了". For example:

火车快来了。(The train is coming.)

天气快冷了。(It is becoming cool.)

▲▼ 2. Can you try?

Steps: (1) Prepare a calendar and vocabulary cards about festivals learned in this lessen. Then make a form to fill them in.

(2) Open the calendar and choose a date close to a festival (e.g., New Year) learned in this lesson and raise it up to ask students "今天几月几日？" Students answer according to the calendar.

(3) Take out the New Year card and lead students to say: "新年快到了。" Then ask "新年你们想做什么？" Students give their answers.

(4) Fill the various answers of the students in the form and find the most popular activity during the festival according to the result.

(5) To continue the game, use another date on the calendar and repeat the above.

▲▼ 3. Let's talk. (CD)

Steps: (1) Students listen to the CD, and then do imitating practice in different roles.

(2) Students come up to the front of the class to perform in groups. Then the teacher comments and appraises.

Translation:

Nancy: Spring festival is coming. What are you going to do?

Jack: I'm going to travel.

Nancy: When are you leaving?

Jack: On Saturday.

Nancy: How about Mingming?

Jack: He wants to see his friends.

4. Do you know? (CD-ROM)

The Spring Festival

The Spring Festival also called the lunar New Year's Day falls on the first day of the first month of the lunar year. It is the most important festival in China. "春节" means winter is over and spring is coming. During this day the Chinese offer sacrifices to the Heaven and the Earth, the gods and ancestors, and pray for abundant harvests of all food crops, good luck in everything.

The Spring Festival is a time for family reunion. No matter how far away they may be, people will try their best to return home to celebrate the festival. On New Year's Eve it is customary for the Chinese to decorate the entrances of their homes with auspicious antithetical couplets, eat dumplings and let off firecrackers to drive off evil and misfortune. They also stick large red Chinese character "福" on the doors of every house spreading festive atmosphere everywhere. Early on the first day of the Lunar New Year people visit their relatives and friends. The children not only put on new clothes and play with firecrackers but also receive red packets or red paper envelopes — enclosed with cash —given to them by elder family members and friends as lunar New Year gifts. Of course the children are the happiest during the Spring Festival!

5. Learn to read. (CD, CD-ROM)

A Tongue Twister
Xiaoshan went mountain-climbing.
Went up the mountain and down the mountain.
Working up a good sweat,
So three shirts got wet.

6. Learn to write. (CD-ROM)

朋

"朋" in ancient times means "two strings of shells" which was used as a measure unit for currency. Later it referred to persons studying under the same master but now it refers to persons having dealings or a friendly relationship with each other.

友

"友" in ancient Chinese resembles two hands stretching at the same time. Two hands intersecting with each other indicate shaking hands to show friendship. The original meaning of "友" has the same meaning which "朋友" (friend) now has. But in ancient times "朋" and "友" differed from each other: persons studying under the same master were called "朋" while persons having a common goal were called "友".

⬍ 7. Let's do it. (CD-ROM)

Hand-torn Lantern

Steps: (1) Fold the paper.

(2) Draw lines on the paper.

(3) Tear it by hands.

(4) Unfold the paper.

⬍ 8. Story time. (CD, CD-ROM)

① Tomorrow is my birthday.

② So many gifts!

③ Mama and papa will be very busy today, so we'll not come home to eat supper.

⑤ Today is my birthday.

⑥ Happy birthday!

WORKBOOK

⬍ 1. Write out the characters below the *pinyin*.

Steps: (1) Students look at the pictures, read the *pinyin* and guess their meanings.

(2) Students write out the Chinese characters according to their meanings. Then count the number of strokes for each character.

⬍ 2. Match them.

Step: Students look at the pictures, then match the portraits with their corresponding Chinese characters and the *pinyin*.

3. Classify and stick.

Steps: (1) Students color the words "春节", and "圣诞节", then tell their meanings.

(2) Students classify the articles on the sticker pages according to the festivals, then stick them in their respective frames.

Answers:

①饺子、红灯笼、福字、鞭炮、对联

②圣诞树、圣诞老人、驯鹿、圣诞袜

4. Listen and fill in the blanks. (CD)

Steps: (1) Students look at the pictures, then read the questions.

(2) Students fill the correct answers in the blanks according to the CD.

CD script:

Jīntiān liù yuè èrshí rì, xiàtiān kuài dào le.
① 今天 6 月 20 日,夏天 快 到 了。

Jīntiān yī yuè shíjiǔ rì, Chūn Jié kuài dào le.
② 今天 1 月 19 日, 春 节 快 到 了。

Jīntiān shí'èr yuè èrshíbā rì, xīnián kuài dào le.
③ 今天 12 月 28 日, 新年 快 到 了。

Jīntiān shí'èr yuè èrshí'èr rì, Shèngdàn Jié kuài dào le.
④ 今天 12 月 22 日, 圣诞 节 快 到 了。

Jīntiān jiǔ yuè shíliù rì, qiūtiān kuài dào le.
⑤ 今天 9 月 16 日, 秋天 快 到 了。

5. Look and tell the differences.

Steps: (1) Students look at the two pictures, then tell the names of these two festivals.

(2) Students tell the differences between the two festivals. The teacher can organize students to discuss first. Then have students answer. Answers in English are also OK.

Answers: ①春节　②圣诞节

6. Interview your classmates.

Steps: (1) Have students go around and interview their classmates according to the picture. The two questions are: "新年你想做什么?" and "什么时候做?"

(2) Ask students to fill out the form according to their answers.

7. Color it and write.

Steps: (1) Students look at the pictures, then choose the crayon colors according to the instruction.

(2) Instruct students to fill the blessing words "春节快乐" in the air bubbles.

HOMEWORK

Ask students to draw their favorite festival pictures and give reasons why they like these festivals during the next class session.

中国国家汉办重点规划教材

汉语乐园

教师用书 3

刘富华　王　巍

周芮安　李冬梅　编著

邵　壮　译

北京语言大学出版社

BEIJING LANGUAGE AND CULTURE
UNIVERSITY PRESS

（京）新登字 157 号

图书在版编目（CIP）数据

汉语乐园教师用书．3／ 刘富华，王巍，周芮安，李冬梅编著．
——北京：北京语言大学出版社，2006 重印
ISBN 7-5619-1438-5

Ⅰ．汉…

Ⅱ．①刘…②王…③周…④李…

Ⅲ．汉语－对外汉语教学－教学参考资料

Ⅳ．H195.4

中国版本图书馆 CIP 数据核字（2005）第 052659 号

北京语言大学出版社
BEIJING LANGUAGE AND CULTURE
UNIVERSITY PRESS

书　　　名：汉语乐园教师用书 3
责任印制：汪学发

出版发行：北京语言大学出版社
社　　　址：北京市海淀区学院路 15 号　　邮政编码：100083
网　　　址：www.blcup.com
电　　　话：发行部 82303648/3591/3651
　　　　　　编辑部 82303647
　　　　　　读者服务部 82303653/3908
印　　　刷：北京画中画印刷有限公司
经　　　销：全国新华书店

版　　　次：2005 年 12 月第 1 版　　2006 年 1 月第 2 次印刷
开　　　本：889 毫米×1194 毫米　1/16　　印张：14.5　　插表：1
字　　　数：211 千字　　　印数：3001-8000
书　　　号：ISBN 7-5619-1438-5/H · 05052
　　　　　　04900

目 录 CONTENTS

使用说明

《汉语乐园》是一套供英语国家小学生使用的初级汉语选修课教材，包括：学生用书6册、活动手册6册、教师用书(中、英文)3册，共15册。

一、教学目标

1. 听懂并会说一些简单的汉语句子。

2. 学会唱一些中文儿童歌曲，并能背诵一些童谣和简单的诗歌。

3. 初步掌握汉字基本知识，如基本笔画、笔顺等，会写一些笔画简单的汉字。

4. 初步了解一点中国文化。

二、编写原则

1. 针对性和科学性原则

本教材针对英语国家小学生课堂上活泼好动、喜欢手工和做游戏等特点，将语言教学、文化介绍和游戏活动三者结合。其中语言教学是基础，文化介绍和游戏活动是两翼，目的是使学生在感性活动中了解汉语、了解中国。教材配有教师用书、CD和CD-ROM等多媒体教学资料，使教材具有多种教学手段。

语言点的编排和语言技能的训练遵循汉语作为第二语言的习得规律。课文、生词和语法点依照由浅入深、循序渐进的原则进行科学的分布和合理的复现；汉字、词语和句子教学则通过生动有趣的形式来

实现。使学生在轻松愉快的气氛中学习汉语，体现本教材"寓教于乐，寓学于乐"的编写理念。

2. 知识性和趣味性原则

以情景话题的编排为例，话题的选择既要考虑交际功能的实用性和语言教学的科学性，还要充分考虑少年儿童活泼好动、好奇心强的特点。为此，选择了一些常用的交际话题，如问候、寒暄、感谢、询问、邀请等；同时也选择了一些小学生感兴趣的话题，如旅游、娱乐、运动、动物等。

为适应小学生活泼好动的特点，学生用书和活动手册采用趣味性强、需要亲手做的练习方式，如手工制作、不干胶贴画等，使语言文化知识的传授和有趣的游戏活动完美结合。

三、教学内容

1. 词汇教学

教材词汇量的确定参考了中国国家对外汉语教学领导小组办公室汉语水平考试部制订的《汉语水平词汇与汉字等级大纲》和澳大利亚等英语国家的小学汉语教学大纲，词汇总量约500个，其中学生用书中的生词为必记词，教师用书中还有若干补充词，配有拼音和英文翻译。

2. 汉字教学

对英语国家的学生来说，汉字是学习的难点。为了克服学生对汉字的畏难情绪，教材做了如下设计：

(1)汉字教学的目标在于培养学生对汉字的兴趣，不要求会写每个汉字，学生能够认读简单汉字，并初步了解汉字的书写规则即可。

(2)学生用书从每课中选取一两个汉字(以象形文字为主)，以图画方式让学生了解汉字的起源和演变，帮助学生认读汉字。

(3)活动手册以剪、贴、画、涂色、添笔画等多种形式练习汉字，避免了写汉字的枯燥和乏味。

(4)学生用书配有图文并茂的词语卡片，帮助教师讲解汉字。

3. 拼音教学

声调配图和拼音背景插图设计是本教材的特色之一，拼音教学中

荣誉证书

右燕 老师指导的 沈思萱 同学写作

的《

法国-尼斯

》一文，荣获

十四届世界华人学生作文大赛三等奖。

世界华人学生作文大赛评委会
二〇一三年五月
评委会

主办单位

中华全国归国华侨联合会
人民日报海外版

中华全国台湾同胞联谊会
中国国际广播电台

《快乐作文》杂志
中央电视台

还穿插了一些童谣、古诗、绕口令，都是为了使拼音教学生动有趣。

对汉语中的语流音变，本教材按实际读音标调，具体说明见教师用书后的《关于〈汉语拼音方案〉》。

4. 语法教学

根据话题，选取基本句型和其他语法点40余个，教师用书对每个语法点都进行了详细的讲解。鉴于学生的接受能力，本教材不建议教师在课堂上讲授语法，语言点讲解仅供教师参考。

5. 文化教学

结合语言教学，选取了小学生感兴趣的中国文化内容，如武术、节日、动物等，使学生对中国的自然地理、历史文化和社会生活有一个初步的了解，调动他们学习汉语的积极性。

6. 游戏活动

本教材在每课的最后设计了一些具有中国文化特点的游戏活动，如踢毽子、学中国功夫等传统的体育活动以及包饺子、剪纸、做风筝等传统的文化活动。

四、教材体例

(一) 学生用书3个级别，6册，每个级别12课。体例如下：

1. Can you say?

包括两个部分：情景会话和生词，生词与情景会话中同一颜色的词语可做替换练习。

2. Can you try?

这是一个互动游戏，让学生和老师一起以游戏方式操练"Can you say?"中的句型和生词。

3. Do you know?

这部分是文化内容，插图中有对本课文化内容的简要说明，通常还包括一个问题，学生会在教师的讲解中找到问题的答案。

4. Learn to read.

在学生用书1中，这部分是汉语拼音；在学生用书2和学生用书3中，这部分是歌谣、古诗、谜语或者绕口令。

5. Let's talk.

这部分是可供学生表演的小对话，只在学生用书3中出现，用来复习已经学过的内容。

6. Learn to write.

这部分是汉字学习。学生用书1和学生用书2每课讲解一个汉字（少数课讲两个汉字），学生用书3平均每课讲解两至三个汉字。

7. Let's do it.

这部分是游戏活动，其中编排了简单有趣的中国传统游戏和手工制作，大部分活动与本课的语言教学内容和文化内容相结合。

8. Let's sing.

中文歌曲，一般编排在每个单元的第二课后边。

9. Story time.

这部分是讲故事，编排在每个单元的第二课后边。以连环画的形式帮助学生复习以前学过的内容，同时也会出现一些新的句子，但不要求学生掌握。

10. Review

每三个单元后有一个复习页，以不干胶贴画的形式帮助学生复习这三个单元的主要句型。

此外，学生用书后边附有生词表。

（二）活动手册

这是本教材的练习用书，与学生用书相配套，3个级别共6册，每个级别12课，每课包括6～8道练习题，第3级别中还增加了一个家庭作业。每课的练习包括语音、汉字、词语、会话四个环节，活动手册后边附有与练习配套的不干胶贴画、描字练习。

（三）教师用书

教师用书共3册，书后附有奖励小彩贴，供教师上课时奖励学生使用。

除上述内容外，本教材还包括如下一些教学附件：

1. 教学备品盒。内有与教材内容配套的美猴王面具、风筝、跳绳、毽子、剪纸、中国结、中国地图等7种具有中国文化特色的小物件。每册书学完后，作为奖励，获得小彩贴最多的学生可以得到其中的一个礼物。

2. CD（随书赠送）。

3. CD-ROM。

4. 字母卡片。

5. 学生用书词语卡片。

6. 教学挂图。

五、教学时间分配

针对英语国家小学汉语教学课时总量少，各学校授课课时不一的情况，本教材在内容编排上体现了机动灵活的特点。课时少的学校可适当减少游戏活动；课时多的学校，可利用教师用书及配套的教学附件多组织一些活动。

具体教学时间如下：

1级　每课需用约4学时。

2级　每课需用约5学时。

3级　每课需用约6学时。

希望《汉语乐园》成为您汉语教学的好帮手！

在教材编写的过程中，鲁健骥、李晓琪、罗青松、朱志平、张健民、刘晓雨等国内高校专家对教材的样课和定稿进行了审定，提出了许多宝贵的意见和建议，在此一并表示感谢。

编者

Lesson 1

春天来了

交际话题：**谈季节**

教学目标：句型： 春天来了。
真暖和！

生词： 春天、夏天、秋天、冬天、
冷、热、暖和、凉快、来、
了、真

汉字： 春、天

文化： 中国的气候

教学备品：(1) 四张代表春、夏、秋、冬的图片。
(2) 风车制作材料：小木棍、硬纸、
图钉。
(3) 中国地图。

1

STUDENT'S BOOK

导入

教师用英语询问当下季节，并提问个别学生"你喜欢什么季节？"按照学生的回答，把春、夏、秋、冬四季图片贴在黑板上。

◆ 1. Can you say? (CD)

会话译文

Spring is coming! It's *warm*!

替换部分译文

① *summer, hot*   ② *autumn, cool*   ③ *winter, cold*

补充词

潮湿	cháoshī	humid
干燥	gānzào	dry

句型讲解

(1) 春天来了。

"了"在本课为语气助词,用在句末,表示事态已经出现变化或将要出现变化。如：

春天来了。

下雨了。

(2) 真暖和！

"真" 在本课为副词,有"实在,的确"之义,通常用于口语,用来加强肯定的语气。如：

真好吃！

真好看！

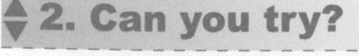

◆ 2. Can you try?

步骤：

（1）教师准备好"春天、夏天、秋天、冬天"四张词语卡片。

（2）教师请几名学生到前面表演。教师举起一张卡片如"冬天"，大声说"冬天来了。"

（3）前面的几名学生立即按听到的内容做出相应的动作，例如表现出冬天冷得发抖的样子。

（4）其他学生根据这几名学生的表演齐声说"真冷！"

◆ 3. Let's talk. (CD)

步骤：

（1）教师介绍人物：小龙、杰克，并按课文中的情节插图用英文讲解对话。

（2）学生听录音，分角色朗读并进行模仿练习(可先准备 5 分钟)。

（3）学生分组上台表演，教师讲评，优秀者可获得小彩贴。

会话译文：

Xiaolong: Autumn is coming.

Jack: The autumn in Beijing is very beautiful!

Xiaolong: Do you like autumn?

Jack: Yes, it is cool.

◆ 4. Do you know? (CD-ROM)

中国的气候

中国的土地辽阔，地形复杂，气候差异很大。在最北端的地区，夏天非常短暂，冬季漫长又寒冷；而地处最南端的海南岛则四季炎热，没有冬天。沿海的东南部地区大部分四季潮湿，而被称为"世界屋脊"的青藏高原则终年冰雪覆盖。所以，即使你在同一个季节走遍全中国，也会感受到不同的四季景致。

游戏： 教师提供四张标有"冷、热、暖和、凉快"的词语卡片，让学生在中国地图上找到冷、热、暖和、凉快的地区，并把相应的词语卡片分别贴入。

▲ 5. Learn to read. (CD,CD-ROM)

▲ 6. Learn to write. (CD-ROM)

天

"天"的本义为人的头部或头顶。早期的"天"字就像一个正面而立的人形，而且特别突出了人的头形，现引申为头顶以上的天空，还可以用来泛指自然界。现在把一昼夜的时间也称为"一天"，如"今天、明天"等等。

▲ 7. Let's do it. (CD-ROM)

做风车

步骤：

(1) 拿出一张正方形硬纸。

(2) 分别把四个角两两对折。

(3) 用剪刀沿对角线从外向里剪，剪至距中心2厘米处。

(4) 把每一个角沿顺时针方向弯向中心。

(5) 用一个图钉把四个角固定于一个木棍上。

(6) 到户外，举着风车逆风行走或奔跑，风车就会旋转起来。

▲ 8. Let's sing. (CD,CD-ROM)

译文：

Where is the Spring

Where is the spring, Where is the spring?

The spring is right in the kids' eyes.

Hare are the red flowers, and there the green grass.

Still there are little orioles that can sing.

Li, li, li....

Li, li, li....

Still there are little orioles that can sing.

Still there are little orioles that can sing.

WORKBOOK

1. Write and say.

步骤：

(1) 学生根据背景图及所给的笔画顺序描、写汉字。

(2) 学生用汉语读出四个季节并翻译。

2. Look and stick.

步骤：

(1) 学生根据自己国家的习惯读温度计（华氏或摄氏）。

华式与摄氏转换公式：

$F = 9 \times C \div 5 + 32$

$C = (F - 32) \times 5 \div 9$

(2) 学生判断冷、热、暖和、凉快，并从不干胶贴页中找到这些词，分别贴入空白处。

3. Color and match them.

步骤：

(1) 学生将词义、音、图连线。

(2) 在教师的提示下，分别选择适合春、夏、秋、冬的颜色为生词涂色。

4. Find, circle and write.

步骤：

(1) 教师指导学生进行朗读、释义。

(2) 学生选出本课学习的与天气有关的词，用彩笔圈上。

(3) 学生根据题下的插图图义，把相应的拼音写在横线上。

答案：

① lěng   ② rè   ③ nuǎnhuo   ④ liángkuai

▼ 5. Listen, choose and color them. (CD)

步骤：

(1) 学生听录音，根据录音内容选择插图。

(2) 学生给插图涂色。

录音文本：

Qiūtiān lái le, zhēn liángkuai!

① 秋天　来了，　真　凉快！

Xiàtiān lái le, zhēn rè!

② 夏天　来了，真　热！

Dōngtiān lái le, zhēn lěng!

③ 冬天　来了，真　冷！

▼ 6. Choose, draw and say.

步骤：

(1) 教师让学生想象一下自己最喜欢的季节，并在所给季节下的小方框中标出。

(2) 让学生在大方框内画出自己最喜欢的季节，并在图中画出穿着当季服装的自己。

(3) 让学生到前面讲一讲自己的作品，优秀者可获得一个小彩贴。

▼ 7. Complete the dialogues.

步骤：

读对话并根据图义完成对话。

答案：

Xǐhuan. Chūntiān hěn nuǎnhuo.

① 喜欢。　春天　很　暖和。

Bù xǐhuan. Xiàtiān hěn rè.

② 不　喜欢。　夏天　很　热。

Xǐhuan. Qiūtiān hěn liángkuai.

③ 喜欢。　秋天　很　凉快。

Bù xǐhuan. Dōngtiān hěn lěng.

④ 不　喜欢。　冬天　很　冷。

步骤：

(1) 学生读图并根据图下提示试说句子。

(2) 教师提问并更正。

答案：

Jiǎozi zhēn hǎochī!

① 饺子　真　好吃！

Míngming de máoyī zhēn dà/cháng!

② 明明　的　毛衣　真　大/长！

Jiékè zhēn gāo!

③ 杰克　真　高！

Tā zhēn ǎi!

④ 他　真　矮！

HOMEWORK

教师让学生利用网络了解一下自己感兴趣的国家的气候情况，下一节课让学生自由发言。

UNIT ONE SEASONS & WEATHER

Lesson 2

今天天气怎么样

交际话题：谈天气

教学目标： 句型：今天天气怎么样？
生词：晴天、阴天、下雨、下雪、
刮风、天气、怎么样
汉字：风、雨
文化：风筝的起源

教学备品： (1) 风衣、太阳镜、雨伞、帽子、手套等。
(2) 代表"晴天""阴天"的两个自制头饰。
(3) 一只风筝。
(4) "剪雪花"所需的一张带颜色的纸、一把
剪刀。

STUDENT'S BOOK

复习与导入

(1) 教师利用卡片，带领学生复习春、夏、秋、冬与冷、热、暖和、凉快等表示季节和天气的词。

(2) 教师打开窗户用英语问："今天天气怎么样？"并拿出代表"晴天"和"阴天"的两个头饰，让学生选择并戴上。

◆ 1. Can you say? (CD)

会话译文

What's the weather like today?

It *rained*.

It's *sunny* today.

替换部分译文

① *snow*   ② *windy*   ③ *cloudy*

补充词

打雷	dǎ léi	thunder
闪电	shǎndiàn	lightning
多云	duōyún	cloudy

句型讲解

今天<u>天气怎么样</u>？

"怎么样"，疑问代词，询问状况，做谓语，相当于英语中的"How (about)...?"如：

明天天气<u>怎么样</u>？

我们去公园<u>怎么样</u>？

▲▼ 2. Can you try?

步骤：

(1) 教师将道具风衣、太阳镜、雨伞、帽子、手套放在桌上。

(2) 教师准备好提示（本课词语卡片"下雨""下雪""刮风""晴天""阴天"）。

(3) 几名学生站在讲台前，教师面对其他学生举起一张词语卡片，让学生根据卡片齐声说（如"下雨了"）。前面的几名学生根据听到的内容找到桌上相关的道具（如雨伞，马上打开撑起），看谁做得最快。

(4) 教师带领学生复习第一课中有关冷、热、暖和、凉快的表达法。

▲▼ 3. Let's talk. (CD)

步骤：

(1) 教师介绍人物：老师、安妮。学生听录音，分角色朗读并进行模仿练习（准备5分钟）。

(2) 学生分组上台表演，教师讲评，优秀者获得小彩贴。

会话译文：

Teacher: What day is today?

Annie: It's Tuesday.

Teacher: What's the weather like today?

Annie: It snowed, very cold.

Teacher: How about tomorrow?

Annie: It will be a sunny day.

▲▼ 4. Do you know? (CD-ROM)

风筝的起源

风筝起源于两千多年前的中国。那时有个聪明人在抬头望天的时候，注意到有一种鹰，它可以长时间一动不动地在天空中翱翔，于是受到启发，依照这种鹰的样子做成了"木风筝"。早期的风筝

非常大，可用来载人或用于军事。后来，随着纸的发明，人们开始用竹子和纸做小一些的风筝。由于制作方法越来越简便，人人都可以做了，于是放风筝就演变成了一种娱乐体育兼备的项目，一直流传到今天。

风筝是一项了不起的发明，要知道飞机的发明也是受了风筝的启发呢！

现在世界各国，喜欢放风筝的人越来越多。中国的潍坊市在1988年4月1日正式被评为"世界风筝之都"，每年都举办一次风筝节。

▲ 5. Learn to read. (CD,CD-ROM)

▲ 6. Learn to write. (CD-ROM)

雨

雨，本义指雨水。甲骨文中的"雨"字，像从天空中降落的雨滴的形状。汉字中凡以"雨"字为偏旁的字大都与云、雨等天文现象有关，可引申为从天空中洒落之义，如：雷（thunder）、雪（snow）、雾（fog）等。

▲ 7. Let's do it. (CD-ROM)

放风筝

步骤：

① 教师拿出风筝，给学生大致讲解风筝的做法。

② 选择风力3~4级的天气，带领学生到一块较为宽敞的草地或广场上。

③ 展开线轴，顺风抛出风筝，边逆风行走边转动手中的线轴，放开线绳，调整角度与高低，使风筝逐渐升高。

▲ 8. Story time. (CD, CD-ROM)

译文：

① How wonderful today's weather is!

② So high! So beautiful!

③ Look! Bverybody likes me!

④ It's raining!

⑤ Help!

WORKBOOK

⬍ 1. Stick and write.

步骤：

(1) 学生试读，教师提问意思。

(2) 根据所给的笔画顺序，学生在不干胶贴页中找到相关的笔画部件分别贴入。

(3) 学生在所给的框中练习写汉字。

⬍ 2. Circle out the correct *pinyin* for each character.

步骤：

(1) 学生根据标志试读每个汉字。

(2) 学生为汉字选择正确读音，大声读出，并翻译。

⬍ 3. Listen, draw and color them. (CD)

步骤：

(1) 学生听录音，为人物画上适当的物品。

(2) 学生为完整的图画涂色。

录音文本：

      Jīntiān qíngtiān.

① 今天　　晴天。

Xià yǔ le.

② 下 雨 了。

Xià xuě le.

③ 下 雪 了。

Guā fēng le.

④ 刮 风 了。

◆ 4. Look and match them.

步骤：

(1) 学生看图，根据图中绘出的天气情况连线。

(2) 学生说出连线内容。

◆ 5. Look and answer.

步骤：

(1) 教师提问："今天天气怎么样？"随后指图①或图②，学生按图回答。

(2) 教师提问："昨天天气怎么样？"随后指图③或图④，让学生按图回答。

◆ 6. Recall the weather for last week.

步骤：

(1) 学生回忆上星期的天气情况。

(2) 从五种天气标识中分别选出合适的选项填入七页空白日历中。

(3) 总结说出从星期一到星期日的天气情况。

◆ 7. Draw and say.

步骤：

(1) 教师引导学生根据当天的天气情况预测第二天的天气。

(2) 学生通过想象画出一幅反映第二天天气的彩图，图内要有当

地标志性建筑。

(3) 学生根据自己的图画说出第二天的天气情况。

▲ 8. Make a flake. (CD-ROM)

步骤：

(1) 拿出准备好的一张带颜色的纸、一把剪刀和一支笔。

(2) 按图示折纸、画线，剪掉多余部分。

(3) 展开即得到一朵六角雪花。

学生为风筝图面涂色，看谁能涂出一个最多彩最像蝴蝶的风筝。（注意蝴蝶的对称性）

UNIT TWO SPORTS & HOBBIES

Lesson 3

你会游泳吗

交际话题：运动

教学目标：句型：你会游泳吗？
　　　　　　　　　我不会。
　　　　　　生词：乒乓球、棒球、网球、篮球、
　　　　　　　　　游泳、滑冰、会、打
　　　　　　汉字：网、球
　　　　　　文化：太极拳

教学备品：(1) 与本课内容有关的运动器具（如乒乓球、
　　　　　　　　篮球、网球等）。
　　　　　　(2) 一副乒乓球拍、球网或绳子、记分牌。

STUDENT'S BOOK

复习与导入

（1）教师检查作业，让学生展示自己的风筝图画，选出最好的给予奖励。

（2）教师和学生谈季节、天气，引出当季大家喜欢的体育运动，写在黑板上。

（3）教师逐一用英语询问学生："你会……吗？"引出本课句型。

▲ 1. Can you say? (CD)

会话译文

Can you *swim*?

I can *swim*.

I can't.

替换部分译文

① *play table tennis*　② *play baseball*

③ *play basketball*　④ *play tennis*　⑤ *skate*

补充词

滑板	huábǎn	skateboard
排球	páiqiú	volleyball
足球	zúqiú	football
橄榄球	gǎnlǎnqiú	rugby

句型讲解

你会游泳吗？

"会"是能愿动词，后接动词，表示有能力做某事或懂得怎样做某事，可以单独回答问题。否定用"不会"。如：

我会说汉语。

我不会打篮球。

"会"也可做动词，后接名词宾语，表示熟悉、通晓。如：

我会汉语。

她会什么？

◆ 2. Can you try?

步骤：

(1) 教师把六个有关运动的词语卡片平行贴在黑板上。

(2) 教师站在第一张卡片（如"棒球"）前问"谁会打棒球？"回答"会"的同学迅速跑到前面在此卡前站成一竖排。

(3) 教师数一下人数，在"棒球"卡下标注人数，然后让学生回到座位上。

(4) 以此类推，得出会每一项运动的人数，学生可多项选择。

(5) 教师引领学生集体总结，分别问会每一类运动的学生："你们会打棒球吗？"学生回答："我们会打棒球。""我们会打乒乓球。"等等。

(6) 同时，教师可引导学生找出最受欢迎的运动项目。

◆ 3. Let's talk. (CD)

步骤：

(1) 学生听录音，跟随教师朗读。

(2) 教师讲解对话，学生分角色朗读并进行模仿练习。

(3) 学生分组表演，教师评优并进行奖励。

会话译文：

Annie and Jack: Hello!

Xiaolong: Hello!

Xiaolong: Where are you going?

Annie and Jack: We are going to play tennis. Will you go with us?

Xiaolong: No, I don't know how to play tennis. I can play table tennis.

▲ **4. Do you know?** (CD-ROM)

太极拳

太极拳是中国拳术的一种，从古至今都是中国人用来锻炼身体和自卫的一种方法。太极拳打起来动作缓慢柔和，讲究心静体松，柔中有刚；要求思想集中，呼吸和动作配合，做到"深、长、习、静"。常打太极拳，对人的大脑、神经、内脏器官都有很好的保健作用。在中国，每天早晚在公园里打太极拳的人可多了，人们都说"常打太极拳，不用上医院"呢！

▲ **5. Learn to read.** (CD, CD-ROM)

▲ **6. Learn to write.** (CD-ROM)

网

网，本义是"捕鱼或鸟兽的工具"。甲骨文中的"网"字，左右两边是木棍，中间是一张网的形状。今天的"网球"就是由场地中间的网状隔断而得名。

▲ **7. Let's do it.** (CD-ROM)

一场乒乓球比赛

乒乓球被称为中国的国球，是中国人非常喜爱的体育运动之一。打乒乓球既可以锻炼身体，也可以锻炼人的反应能力，使人思维灵活、敏捷。另外，这种运动需要的场地较小，设备也很简单，而且不受天气的限制，所以越来越受到人们的欢迎。

步骤：

① 室内、室外均可，如没有乒乓球案，教师可带领学生用八张桌子拼成一个简单的球案，中间用球网隔开。

② 通过教师讲解或看CD-ROM了解规则，即5局3胜或7局4胜，每局11分，每两球换发一次，发球飞出对方球案为失分。

③ 教师组织学生按规则练习发球（两人、四人均可）。

④ 组织比赛，教师充当裁判与记分员。

⑤ 奖励胜方小彩贴。

◆ 8. Let's sing. (CD,CD-ROM)

译文：

A Doll Is Dancing with a Little Bear

A doll is dancing with a little bear, dancing and dancing, yee-yee-oh.

A doll is dancing with a little bear, dancing and dancing, yee-yee-oh.

A doll is dancing with a little bear, dancing and dancing, yee-yee-oh.

A doll is dancing with a littlc bcar, dancing and dancing, yee-yee-oh.

◆ 1. Join the dots and write.

步骤：

(1) 学生试读，教师提问汉字的意思。

(2) 学生把球拍中用虚线写的汉字描实。

(3) 在另一副球拍空白处学写这两个汉字。

◆ 2. Match them.

步骤：

(1) 学生试读并了解"打"的词义和词性。

(2) 学生将动词"打"与可以跟它相搭配的图片用线连起来。

(3) 教师领读出正确的动宾搭配。

答案:

dǎ   bàngqiú /wǎngqiú / lánqiú /pīngpāngqiú

打　　棒球／　　网球／　　篮球／　　乒乓球

◆ 3. Write *pinyin*, match and color them.

（1）学生为每个汉字卡片标出拼音。

（2）学生看彩图，根据图义将每一幅图与生词连线。

（3）学生按照每幅彩图为相对应的黑白图涂色。

◆ 4. Listen and tick. (CD)

步骤:

（1）学生听两遍录音，根据录音内容选择正确的图片。

（2）教师提问，学生复述听到的内容。

录音文本:

Jiékè huì dǎ pīngpāngqiú.

① 杰克　会　打　　乒乓球。

Xiǎolóng bú huì yóuyǒng.

② 小龙　　不会　游泳。

Wǒ xǐhuan dǎ lánqiú.

③ 我　喜欢　打　篮球。

答案: ①A　②B　③A

◆ 5. Find and say.

步骤:

（1）学生从左端人物图像开始沿线行进找到右端与之相对的运动图片。

（2）学生在横线上用拼音或汉字写出运动名称。

答案:

huá bīng　　　　　dǎ wǎngqiú　　　　　dǎ pīngpāngqiú

安妮：滑冰　方方：打网球　圆圆：打乒乓球

yóuyǒng　　　　　dǎ bàngqiú

杰克：游泳　小龙：打棒球

6.Complete the dialogue.

步骤：

(1) 学生看图，根据图义完成对话。

(2) 教师提问并给出正确答案。

答案：

Nǐ huì dǎ pīngpāngqiú ma?

杰克：你 会 打 乒乓球 吗？

Bú huì.

小龙：不 会。

Nǐ huì dǎ lánqiú ma?

杰克：你 会 打 篮球 吗？

Huì, wǒ xǐhuan dǎ lánqiú

小龙：会， 我 喜欢 打 篮球。

Hǎo! Wǒmen qù dǎ lánqiú.

杰克：好！ 我们 去 打 篮球 。

7. Ask, stick and say.

步骤：

(1) 学生用汉语分别问旁边的同学（一男一女两位）："你喜欢什么季节、衣服、天气、运动和食物？"

(2) 被问的学生在不干胶贴页中找到能表示自己答案的贴画贴在表格中。

(3) 教师让学生用汉语说明自己的表格内容。

 HOMEWORK

根据文化部分的展示，学生发挥自己的想象力，为太极图涂上自己喜欢的颜色，感受自然的气氛与力量，下一节课前选出最佳作品五幅贴于黑板上。

UNIT TWO SPORTS & HOBBIES

Lesson 4

我喜欢唱歌儿

交际话题：爱好

教学目标：句型：我喜欢唱歌儿，你呢？
生词：画画儿、唱歌、跳舞、看电影、
玩儿电子游戏、听音乐、呢
汉字：画、电
文化：书法和中国画

教学备品：(1) 笔、墨汁、水彩、旧报纸或宣纸。
(2) 两个纸杯、一把大米、塑胶带。

 **STUDENT'S BOOK**

复习与导入

(1) 教师检查涂色作业，评选五幅优秀作品贴在黑板上。

(2) 复习"我会游泳。"等上一课的语言点，并利用词语卡片复习运动类的生词。

(3) 教师利用运动类生词引出本课话题，如拿出词语卡片说"我喜欢游泳"，随即指向一名学生，提问："你呢？"引出本课语言点。

◆ 1. Can you say? (CD)

会话译文

I like *singing*, and *you*?

I like *dancing*.

替换部分译文

① *draw pictures*   ② *play electronic games*

④ *listen to the music*   ③ *see movies*

补充词

看动画片	kàn dònghuàpiàn	see cartoon movie
做运动	zuò yùndòng	do sports

句型讲解

<u>我喜欢</u>唱歌儿，<u>你呢</u>？

动词"喜欢"可以带名词性宾语，如"我喜欢狗。"也可以带动词性宾语，如"我喜欢唱歌儿。""呢"是语气助词，可以在名词、代词等后边构成单部问句，询问"怎么样"。如：

我很好，你呢？（＝你好吗？）

我喜欢吃饺子，你呢？（＝你喜欢吃什么？你喜欢吗？）

我去学校，你呢？（＝你去哪儿？你去吗？）

◆ 2.Can you try?

步骤：

(1) 教师带领学生在户外草地上或教室内围坐一圈。

(2) 教师将本课词语卡片随意放在师生所围坐的圆圈中间。

(3) 教师走到中间拿起一张有关自己爱好的卡片高声对右手边的学生A说："我喜欢××，你呢，A？"

(4) 被问的学生A立刻走到中间，选出写有自己爱好的卡片大声回答"我喜欢××。"然后问右手边的学生B同样的问题"你呢，B？"B学生回答并以此类推，将问题传下去。

(5) 回答时停顿或者出错的学生，要举起表示自己爱好的卡片边读边绕场一周，之后游戏继续进行。

◆ 3. Let's talk. (CD)

步骤：

(1) 教师介绍人物：方方、安妮。学生听录音，分角色朗读对话，并进行模仿练习。

(2) 学生分组表演，表演优秀的学生可得到一个小彩贴。

译文：

Fangfang: What 's your hobby?

　　Annie: I like drawing, how about you?

Fangfang: I don't like it, I like playing electronic games.

　　Annie: How about Jack?

Fangfang: He likes skating.

4. Do you know? (CD-ROM)

书法和国画

书法和国画是中国流传已久的艺术形式。

书法是一门古老的艺术，自文字产生起它便应运而生。它不仅仅是写字的方法，更是凭借线条和形体结构来表现人的气质、品格、情操的艺术。随着书法历史的发展，先后出现了篆书、隶书、草书、行书、楷书等多种字体，以及多种多样的书法流派。

国画不同于西洋画，它是中国人独特的审美方式和审美习惯的体现。它强调"神似"，不强调"形似"，也不强调光、色的变化。中国画一般分为人物、山水、花鸟三大类。

书法与国画的创作过程中运用的工具——笔、墨、纸、砚都与今天的文具有所不同。笔叫"毛笔"，笔身是用竹子做成的，笔尖由兔、狼等动物的毫毛制成；"墨"就是墨汁，颜色乌黑，由自然界的矿物质制成；"纸"也不同于一般的白纸，是用稻草等材料加工而成的，具有很强的吸水性；"砚"是研磨制作墨汁的容器，是用石头做的，形状各不相同。古代中国称这些东西为"文房四宝"。

5. Learn to read. (CD,CD-ROM)

6. Learn to write. (CD-ROM)

7. Let's do it. (CD-ROM)

画一张简单的国画：燕子

步骤：

① 准备好毛笔、墨、水彩、宣纸（或旧报纸）。

② 教师简单示范执笔法，调墨、蘸墨、运笔动作。

③ 用浓墨画燕子的头和背，重墨画燕子的翅和尾，淡墨勾出燕子的胸部，最后画红颈、黑眼，用浓墨画嘴。

④ 在画儿的左下角署上名字，并写上作画的时间。

Lesson 4 我喜欢唱歌儿

▲▼ 8. Story time. (CD,CD-ROM)

译文:

① What do you go in for?

② I like singing.

Wonderful!

③ I like drawing.

④ I can swim.

I can play basketball.

⑤ How about you, little bear?

I...

⑥ He like sleeping!

WORKBOOK

▲▼ 1. Write.

步骤:

(1) 学生看图,思考本题要求写出的汉字。

(2) 学生为两个"田"字分别填上所缺笔画,使字义与图义相符。

▲▼ 2. Find and write.

步骤:

(1) 教师领读图中的名词或名词性短语,并让学生猜测词义。

(2) 学生为动词找到相应的宾语搭配。

(3) 教师提问并纠错。

答案:

huà huàr   tīng yīnyuè   kàn diànyǐng

① 画 画儿   ② 听 音乐   ③ 看 电影

wánr diànzǐ yóuxì   chàng gēr   tiào wǔ

④ 玩儿 电子 游戏   ⑤ 唱 歌儿   ⑥ 跳 舞

3. Match them.

步骤：

(1) 学生朗读拼音。

(2) 学生根据拼音找到对应的汉字、英译和图片。

4. Look and answer . (CD)

步骤：

(1) 教师指图，读A部分并提问。

(2) 学生看图，根据内容回答问题。

答案： Ānni xǐhuan chàng gēr.

① 安妮 喜欢 唱 歌儿。

　　Xiǎolóng xǐhuan huà huàr.

② 小龙 喜欢 画 画儿。

　　Dìdi xǐhuan wánr diànzǐ yóuxì.

③ 弟弟 喜欢 玩儿 电子 游戏。

5. Listen and stick. (CD)

步骤：

(1) 学生听录音，根据听到的内容找到图中人物身边所缺的乐器
及工具。

(2) 学生从不干胶贴页中找到相应的贴画，将其贴到正确位置。

(3) 做得又快又好的学生可以得到一个小彩贴。

录音文本：

　　Fāngfang xǐhuan chàng gēr.

① 方方 喜欢 唱 歌儿。

　　Ānni xǐhuan tiào wǔ

② 安妮 喜欢 跳 舞。

　　Jiékè xǐhuan huà huàr.

③ 杰克 喜欢 画 画儿。

Xiǎolóng xǐhuan   tīng yīnyuè.

④ 小龙   喜欢   听 音乐。

Míngming xǐhuan   wánr diànzǐ yóuxì.

⑤ 明明   喜欢   玩儿 电子 游戏。

6. Answer the questions according to the picture.

步骤：

(1) 学生朗读提示句，读出问题。

(2) 学生根据图义找出答案并回答。

答案：

Bàba bù xǐhuan hē kělè.

① 爸爸 不 喜欢 喝 可乐。

Gēge xǐhuan yóuyǒng.

② 哥哥 喜欢 游泳。

Māma xǐhuan kàn diànshì.

③ 妈妈 喜欢 看 电视。

Dìdi xǐhuan dǎ pīngpāngqiú.

④ 弟弟 喜欢 打   乒乓球。

7. Make a shaker. (CD-ROM)

步骤：

(1) 找两个同样大小的纸杯，并准备一把大米。

(2) 把大米倒入纸杯，把两杯口对上，用透明胶带把两杯口连接
    处贴牢。

(3) 在空白的杯体上画上自己喜欢的图案（可以画水彩画），签
    上名字。

(4) 下课后拿起来摇动玩耍。

 **HOMEWORK**

这是一个分小组进行的作业，首先教师让学生们通过小组讨论获知对方的爱好，然后让每个学生在纸上画出自己和自己的爱好，再由组长统一收集装成小册子。第二天在班上做集体展示，教师从中评优奖励。

Lesson 5

我要买巧克力

交际话题：购物

教学目标：句型：你要买什么?
　　　　　　　　我要买巧克力和饼干。
　　　　　生词：巧克力、饼干、冰淇淋、糖、
　　　　　　　　薯片儿、汉堡包、三明治、要、
　　　　　　　　买、和
　　　　　汉字：买、和
　　　　　文化：西式快餐在中国

教学备品：(1) 学过的有关食物、饮料、文具的词语卡片。
　　　　　(2) 与本课相关的零食实物、售货员的围裙。
　　　　　(3) 筷子、花生米。

STUDENT'S BOOK

复习与导入

（1）教师检查作业"Make a book"，让学生按小组到教室前展示作品。学生指着画中的自己说"我喜欢……"，以此复习前一课有关爱好的内容。

（2）教师装扮成售货员，拿出准备好的各种零食实物，让学生猜今天学习的内容，从而引出本课话题。

◆ 1. Can you say? (CD)

会话译文

What do you want to buy?

I want to buy *chocolate* and *biscuits*.

替换部分译文

①*ice cream* ②*hamburger* ③*sandwich* ④*candy* ⑤*chips*

补充词

香肠	xiāngcháng	sausage
鸡蛋	jīdàn	egg
口香糖	kǒuxiāngtáng	chewing gum
比萨饼	bǐsàbǐng	pizza

句型讲解

（1）你<u>要</u>买什么？

"要"是助动词，表示做某事的意志。一般不单独回答问题。如：

你要去哪儿？

我要吃饺子。

另外，"你要买什么？"也是中国的售货员招呼顾客的常用

语，相当于 "Can I help you?" 或 "What can I do for you?"

(2) 我要买巧克力和饼干。

"和"，连词，常常连接同类的名词、名词性短语和代词，表示并列关系。"和"连接三个或更多的词或短语时，一般用在最后的词或短语前。如：

我吃饼干和薯片儿。

我有书、笔和本子。

2. Can you try?

步骤：

(1) 教师带领学生把教室的桌子集中到一起，把写有零食名称的生词卡，连同学过的写有饮料、文具的词语卡片一起摆在桌面上，让学生围桌坐下。

(2) 教师扮演售货员，快速问一个学生："你要买什么，A？"学生A必须马上回答。其他学生根据A的回答快速用手拍相应的卡片，第一个拍到正确卡片的学生把卡片拿在手中。

(3) 教师继续问学生B、学生C，以此类推，直到卡片被抢完为止。获得最多卡片的学生可以得到实物奖励。

3. Let's talk. (CD)

步骤：

(1) 教师进行人物介绍：安妮、方方。学生听录音，分角色朗读并进行模仿练习。

(2) 学生分组表演，教师讲评并奖励。

译文：

Fangfang: Where are you going, Annie?

Annie: I am going to the supermarket.

Fangfang: I am going to the shop. What do you want to buy, Annie?

Annie: I want to buy a hamburger, and you?

Fangfang: I want to buy a bag and a pencil.
Annie & Fangfang: Good-bye.

▲ 4. Do you know? (CD-ROM)

西式快餐在中国

中国是个"饮食大国"，虽然中国菜的种类已经多得让人眼花缭乱，但西式快餐一登陆中国，立刻受到了同样热烈的欢迎，尤其是受到了青少年朋友们的喜爱。上世纪80年代末，麦当劳、肯德基等快餐店进入中国，短短十几年的工夫，就已经家喻户晓，无人不知了。今天，它们的连锁店已经遍布中国各大城市。

为什么小小的汉堡包、炸薯条如此深受青少年的喜爱呢？据调查，原因是那里服务快捷、干净卫生、环境舒适；而且它处处为儿童考虑，有游乐区可以玩耍，有流行的玩具赠送。除此以外，在这些地方还可以学习、做功课、开生日派对等等。虽然家长们不太赞成孩子们吃太多的油炸食物，但小朋友们还是乐此不疲。不信你看，只要一到周末，麦当劳和肯德基都会人流不息，几乎是最热闹的餐厅呢！

▲ 5. Learn to read. (CD,CD-ROM)

▲ 6. Learn to write. (CD-ROM)

买

古文中的"买"字，是从网中取贝的意思。"贝"是古代的货币，可以用来换取货物。今天的"买"是一种拿钱换取货物的行为，与"卖"相对。

▲ 7.Let's do it. (CD-ROM)

筷子游戏——夹花生米比赛

筷子在中国已经有三千多年的历史了。远古时代，人们吃食物是用手抓的，发现了火以后，人们没有办法直接拿取发烫的食物，于是就用木棍来帮忙，久而久之，练就了用木棍取食物的本领，这就是筷

子的由来。筷子使用灵活，简单方便，中国菜里的面条、火锅、饺子等食物，只有筷子才能应对自如。现在全世界有超过15亿的人都在使用筷子。

步骤：

① 教师教学生使用筷子的正确姿势动作。

② 将学生分为两人一组进行夹花生米比赛，一分钟内夹取最多者为赢家。

③ 采用淘汰制，选出全班用筷子用得最好的学生。

▲▼ 8.Let's sing. (CD, CD-ROM)

译文：

A Song from a Newspaper Boy

La-la-la,la-la-la, I'm a little newspaper boy.

Start my work in the early morning.

One newspaper, another newapaper,

Today's news is really good.

And you can get two newspapers only for one coin.

▲▼ 1. Write.

步骤：

(1) 学生认读汉字。

(2) 学生根据所给的笔画顺序把笔画虚线描实。

(3) 学生在后面的米字框中练写汉字，查出笔画数，并填入方框中。

2. Find out and write.

步骤：

(1) 学生根据所给的词语寻找相应的拼音。

(2) 学生将相应的拼音写在汉字上方。

答案：

     shǔpiànr   bīngqílín   hànbǎobāo   táng

 ① 薯片儿   ② 冰淇淋   ③ 汉堡包   ④ 糖

     qiǎokèlì   bǐnggān

 ⑤ 巧克力   ⑥ 饼干

3. Match them.

步骤：

(1) 学生试读左列生词。

(2) 学生根据插图和译文进行连线。

4. Read, draw and say.

步骤：

(1) 教师领读超市图中能看到的食物。

(2) 学生根据自己的喜好，选择五种自己喜欢的食品画到购物车中。

(3) 学生涂色，并大声读出自己喜欢的食品的名称。

5. Listen , tick and color them. (CD)

步骤：

(1) 学生听两遍录音。根据录音内容选择正确的插图。

(2) 教师提问，学生为正确的插图涂色。

录音文本：

        Ānni yào mǎi kělè.

① 安妮　要　买 可乐。

        Jiékè yào mǎi hànbǎobāo.

② 杰克　要　买　　汉堡包。

        Xiǎolóng yào mǎi táng.

③ 小龙　　　要 买　糖　。

        Míngming yào mǎi shǔpiànr hé guǒzhī.

④ 明明　　　要　买　薯片儿　和　果汁。

6. Repeat and expand the sentence.

步骤：

(1) 教师示范，朗读第一句。

(2) 学生一个接一个地进行句子扩展，注意"和"的位置。

7. Complete the dialogue.

步骤：

学生按图义读对话，填入所缺部分。

答案：

        Xiǎolóng, nǐ hǎo!

安妮：小龙，　你　好！

        Nǐ hǎo, Ānni!

小龙：你　好，　安妮！

        Nǐ qù nǎr?

安妮：你 去 哪儿?

        Wǒ qù shāngdiàn.

小龙：我　去　商店。

        Nǐ yào mǎi shénme?

安妮：你　要　买　什么?

        Wǒ yào mǎi bǐ hé běnzi.

小龙：我　要　买　笔　和　本子。

HOMEWORK

学生做一个调查统计，找出本班6～10个学生最喜欢的三种食品。下一次上课时由老师作最后统计，找出排在前三名的食品。

UNIT THREE SHOPPING

Lesson 6

多少钱

交际话题：询问价格

教学目标：句型：一斤苹果多少钱？
五元。
生词：苹果、梨、香蕉、西瓜、菠萝、
多少、钱、元、斤
汉字：苹、果
文化：中国古代的计算工具——算盘

教学备品：（1）数字卡片0～9。
（2）可能找到的水果实物或卡片。
（3）售货员围裙、算盘。

复习与导入

(1) 教师检查作业，与学生一起统计"学生们最喜欢的三种食物"。

(2) 一名学生扮演售货员，利用上一课所学的词语问教师："您要买什么？"教师指着一张卡片回答"我买××。"然后教师问："一斤××多少钱？"并在黑板上写出标价，让学生猜出句子的意思，引出本课话题。

◆ 1. Can you say? (CD)

会话译文

How much is half a kilo of *apples*?

Five yuan.

替换部分译文

① *pear, one* ② *watermelon, five*

③ *banana, two* ④ *pineapple, ten*

补充词

桃	táo	peach
葡萄	pútao	grape
草莓	cǎoméi	strawberry
杏	xìng	apricot
樱桃	yīngtao	cherry
枣	zǎo	date

参考游戏1

一个学生站在讲台上，背对着其他同学。在这个学生的后背贴上本课的一个词语，教师给些暗示，让学生猜出是哪个词。每个学生有三次机会，如果回答错误，由其他学生大声纠正，回答正确者获得小彩贴。

参考游戏2

这是一个分组游戏，两人一组，两个学生用词语接龙的方法说出已学过的食品或水果类词语，说得多的学生获胜。

句型讲解：

(1) 一斤苹果<u>多少</u>钱？

"多少"是疑问代词，用来询问数量或者价格。询问数量时一般用于提问"十"以上的数字；询问价格时可直接问"多少钱？"如：

你们班有多少个学生？

一个汉堡包多少钱？

"斤"是重量单位，1斤等于500克。

(2) <u>五元</u>。

"元"是量词，是人民币的基本单位。口语中也可以说"块"。

▼ 2. Can you try?

步骤：

(1) 教师把所学的有关水果的卡片贴在黑板上，每个卡片下面分别用数字标明价格。

(2) 教师找一个学生A，让他随意找另一名同学B互相提问，问题如：A问"一斤西瓜多少钱？"B回答"五元。"A紧接着再问"二斤西瓜多少钱？"B需马上反应，回答出钱数。A可以逐渐提高难度，问"一斤西瓜和三斤香蕉多少钱？"争取把对方难倒。

(3) 由学生B发问，问题同上，游戏进行到一方出错为止。

(4) 答得最快、算得最准的学生可以得到一个小彩贴。

▲ 3.Let's talk. (CD)

步骤：

(1) 学生听录音，分角色朗读并进行模仿练习。

(2) 学生分组表演，教师奖励优秀。

译文：

> Shop assistant: Hello!What can I do for you?
>
> Fangfang: I like to buy apples and pears.
>
> How much is half-kilo of apples?
>
> Shop assistant: Four yuan.
>
> Fangfang: How much is half-kilo of pears?
>
> Shop assistant: Three yuan.
>
> Fangfang: I want to buy half-kilo of apples and half-kilo of pears.
>
> Shop assistant: Seven yuan.

4.Do you know? (CD-ROM)

算盘——古老的计算器

算盘是最古老的计算器，是由中国人的祖先发明的。

古时候，人们用小木棍进行计算，叫做筹算。后来随着生产的发展，粮食多了，牲畜多了，小木棍不够用了，人们就用各种颜色的珠子进行计算。

珠子滚来滚去，使用起来不方便，人们就把珠子穿在木棍上，再用一个木框固定起来，这样算盘就诞生了。算盘制作简单、成本低、计算效果好，而且携带方便、节约能源。

使用算盘需要脑、眼、手密切配合，是锻炼大脑的好方法。使用算盘熟练的人的计算速度可以和计算器的计算速度相媲美呢！

5. Learn to read. (CD, CD-ROM)

6. Learn to write. (CD-ROM)

果

果，在甲骨文中像一颗树上结满果实，它的本义是指"树木所结之实"，后引申为事物的结局。如：结果（result or outcome）。

▼ **7. Let's do it.** (CD-ROM)

游戏:

传话。看哪一组同学能在最短时间内把字条上的词语准确无误地从尾传到头。

步骤:

① 教师将学生分成两排, 每排6~10人。

② 教师提前准备好小纸条, 上面写有四组词语。如: 梨、苹果、香蕉、西瓜或一斤苹果、二斤西瓜、三斤香蕉、四斤梨。

③ 教师把小纸条展示给队尾的同学看, 从该学生开始以悄悄话的形式把纸条上的内容依次向前面的学生传。要求传话的过程中不能偷看, 不能大声说话。

④ 传到最前面的一个学生。教师请他说出纸条上的内容或从词语卡片中找到所传的词语, 并按正确顺序将其贴在黑板上。

⑤ 做得又快又准的一排学生得到奖励。

▲ **8.Story time.** (CD, CD-ROM)

译文:

① How much is a watermelon?

Six yuan.

② A watermelon, please.

③ An apple, please.

④ A peach, please.

⑤ Here is a peach for you.

⑥ Oh? Where is the fruit?

WORKBOOK

▲ **1. Add the missing parts to the charaters.**

步骤:

(1) 学生看图, 读出果实中的汉字。

(2) 学生找出缺失部首或笔画的汉字, 并补充完整。

2. Write the tone mark for each *pinyin* and draw.

步骤：

(1) 学生读拼音，填声调。

(2) 学生根据声调猜词义。

(3) 学生根据词义画相应物品。

3. Count the numbers.

步骤：

学生看图，数出每种食物的数量，并用汉字或拼音填入括号中。

答案： liù   sān   wǔ   jiǔ   shí   sì

① 六 ② 三 ③ 五 ④ 九 ⑤ 十 ⑥ 四

4. Listen, match and say. (CD)

步骤：

(1) 学生说出图画所表示的生词。

(2) 学生听录音，连线。

(3) 教师纠错，给出正确答案。

录音文本：

Shūbāo èrshíbā yuán. Bǐ shíqī yuán.

① 书包　二十八　元。　笔　十七　元。

Màozi shí'èr yuán.　Wàzi bā yuán.

② 帽子　十二　元。　袜子　八　元。

Máoyī liùshí　yuán.　Hànbǎobāo　shí yuán.

③ 毛衣　六十　元。　　汉堡包　　十　元。

Bīngqílín yì yuán. Xiāngjiāo wǔ yuán. Xīguā sān yuán.

④ 冰淇淋　一元。　香蕉　　五　元。西瓜　三　元。

5. Listen and stick. (CD)

步骤：

(1) 学生读英文，理解问题。

(2) 学生听录音，根据录音内容在不干胶贴页中找到相关贴画，
贴入大"书包"内。

录音文本：

shū, bǐ, běnzi, píngguǒ hé lí.
书，笔，本子， 苹果 和 梨。

🔺 6. Fill in the blanks.

步骤：

(1) 学生理解四幅图的含义。

(2) 学生阅读对话，填入所缺的部分。

(3) 教师提问，给出正确答案。

(4) 学生可分角色进行对话练习。

答案：

	Nǐmen hǎo! Nǐmen mǎi shénme?
Shop assistant:	你们 好！你们 买 什么？

	Yì jīn píngguǒ duōshao qián?
方方：	一 斤 苹果 多少 钱？

	Wǔ yuán.
Shop assistant:	五 元 。

	Yì jīn xiāngjiāo duōshao qián?
妈妈：	一 斤 香蕉 多少 钱？

	Sān yuán.
Shop assistant:	三 元。

	Wǒ mǎi yì jīn píngguǒ hé èr jīn xiāngjiāo.
妈妈：	我 买 一 斤 苹果 和 二 斤 香蕉

	Shíyī yuán.
Shop assistant:	十一 元。

7. Look and say.

步骤：

（1）学生在1分钟内看图，尽可能多地记住隐藏在各个角落的词语。

（2）学生合上书，教师提问。说出词语最多的学生可以得到奖励小彩贴。

8. How many things can you buy?

步骤：

（1）学生认读每一种商品的名称和价格。

（2）学生尝试用50元钱购买尽可能多的商品，或者正好花完这些钱。

（3）学生把商品名称和价格一一列在表中，最后计算出总额。

HOMEWORK

结合本课的文化知识，学生发挥想象力，想象并设计出未来的计算机模样。

UNIT FOUR DAILY LIFE

Lesson 7

我今天有汉语课

交际话题：学校生活

教学目标：句型：你今天有什么课？
　　　　　　　　我今天没有课。
　　　　　生词：数学、历史、英语、汉语、体育、
　　　　　　　　地理、课、没有
　　　　　汉字：体、育
　　　　　文化：中国小学生的课程

教学备品：(1) 本班的课表。
　　　　　　(2) 自制骰子，六个面分别写上本课学习的六
　　　　　　　　个科目。
　　　　　　(3) 剪刀、胶水、硬纸板、彩笔。
　　　　　　(4) 每个科目的卡片各五张。

STUDENT'S BOOK

复习与导入

(1) 教师检查作业：让学生展示对未来计算机的描绘图，并让学生说说自己的设计思路。

(2) 教师用英语问学生当天的课程，学生一边回答教师一边写在黑板上，引出本课话题。

1. Can you say? (CD)

会话译文

What classes do you have today?

I have *Chinese* today.

I have no class today.

替换部分译文

①*maths* ②*PE* ③*history* ④*English* ⑤*geography*

补充词

生物	shēngwù	biology
自然	zìrán	nature
手工	shǒugōng	handwork

句型讲解

(1) 我今天有汉语课。

状语是限制、修饰谓语的词或短语，放在被限制、修饰的中心语前面。这个句子中的"今天"是表示时间的前加成分，叫做时间状语。时间状语可放在主语前，也可以放在主语后。如：

昨天她去商店了。

我明天有数学课。

(2) 我今天<u>没有</u>课。

"没有"是动词"有"的否定形式，在这里指对领有、具有的否定。如：

我没有汉语书。

房间里没有电视。

◆ 2. Can you try?

设计课程表

步骤：

(1) 教师在黑板上画一张放大的空课程表，同时准备多张可粘贴的课程卡片。

(2) 教师和学生一起做一个大骰子（六个面分别写上本课学习的六门课）。

(3) 教师提问"你们星期一有什么课？"让一个学生掷骰子决定，教师或学生把掷骰子得到的结果用卡片的形式贴到黑板上的空课表里。

(4) 继续提问，继续掷骰子，贴课表，把一个星期的课程表贴满后，学生便得到了一个自己设计的课程表。

(5) 教师可用英语问学生"你们喜欢自己设计的课程表吗？"如果答案是否定的，教师带领学生把课程表重贴或还原成现在的课程表。

◆ 3.Let's talk. (CD)

步骤：

(1) 教师进行人物介绍：小龙、安妮，他们在校门口。

(2) 学生听录音，教师领读，学生跟读并进行模仿练习。

(3) 教师讲解并翻译，学生分角色表演。

译文：

Xiaolong: Do you have PE class today?

Annie: No.

Xiaolong: What classes do you have today?

Fangfang: Chinese, history and music.

Xiaolong: What classes do you have tomorrow?

Fangfang: It will be Saturday tomorrow, and we have no classes.

4.Do you know? (CD-ROM)

中国小学生的课程

中国孩子的教育从小学正式开始。中国小学生的课程很丰富，主要有数学、语文、英语、历史、地理、自然、政治、音乐、体育、美术等。小学低年级的生活是轻松快乐的，进入五、六年级后，为了升入重点中学，每天的学习变得紧张起来，美术、体育等课程开始逐渐减少，学生的压力也越来越大，快乐的童年生活也渐渐结束在美好的回忆里……

5. Learn to read. (CD, CD-ROM)

6. Learn to write. (CD-ROM)

7. Let's do it. (CD-ROM)

做一个立体课表

步骤：

① 选一张长方形硬纸卡，折成四份，中间两部分大些，相等；两侧部分小些，相等。

② 在中间两部分上分别画出课表和漂亮的图案。

③ 将两侧部分粘在一起，形成一个横放的柱体。

④ 做成了一个立体课表。

♦ 8. Let's sing. (CD, CD-ROM)

译文：

So Many Cattle

So many cattle, so many cattle, the cattle dot the slope.

They are eating fresh grass, and

they are listening to pastoral songs.

♦ 1. Write and classify.

步骤：

(1) 学生试读，根据所给的笔画顺序，在下面框格内学写汉字。

(2) 学生在不干胶贴页中找出属于"体育"的活动，分别贴入六个圆圈中。

♦ 2. Match them and write.

步骤：

(1) 学生朗读每个本子上的汉字。

(2) 学生搭配成词并连线。

(3) 学生把连线的词语写到下面的横线上。

答案：

yīnyuè	Hànyǔ	tǐyù	dìlǐ	lìshǐ	shùxué
①音乐	②汉语	③体育	④地理	⑤历史	⑥数学

♦ 3. Color them and write.

步骤：

(1) 学生为各色小鱼找到搭配项，并涂上相同颜色。

(2) 学生根据气泡内的词义把相应的拼音写在小鱼下的括号里。

答案：

          tǐyù   lìshǐ   Hànyǔ

P.E→体育；history→历史；Chinese→汉语

          shùxué   yīnyuè   Yīngyǔ   dìlǐ

maths→数学；music→音乐；English→英语   geography—地理

4. Find and say.

步骤：

（1）学生从 start 开始进行，遇到图画便联想出相应课程。

（2）学生大声说出课程名称，教师纠错。

答案：

yīnyuè kè tǐyù kè Yīngyǔ kè lìshǐ kè

音乐   课→体育 课→英语   课→历史   课

shùxué kè Hànyǔ kè   dìlǐ kè

→数学   课→ 汉语   课→地理 课

5. Listen and fill in the blanks. (CD)

步骤：

学生读表后，听录音，根据听到的内容填上课程名称。

录音文本：

        Bā diǎn yǒu shùxué kè, jiǔ diǎn yǒu Yīngyǔ kè,

星期一：8   点 有   数学 课，9 点   有   英语课，

        shí diǎn yǒu lìshǐ kè, shíyī diǎn yǒu tǐyù kè.

      10   点   有 历史课，11   点 有 体育 课。

        Bā diǎn yǒu Hànyǔ kè, jiǔ diǎn yǒu yīnyuè kè,

星期二：8 点   有   汉语课，9 点   有   音乐   课，

        shí diǎn yǒu shùxué kè,shíyī diǎn yǒu dìlǐ kè.

      10   点   有   数学 课，11   点 有 地理 课。

⬥ 6. Look and answer.

步骤：

学生读课表后，逐一回答问题。

答案：

　　　Méiyǒu.

① 没有　。

　　　Yǒu.

② 有。

　　　Yǒu Yīngyǔ kè, shùxué kè, Hànyǔ kè hé tǐyù kè.

③ 有　英语　课、数学　课、汉语　课 和 体育 课。

　　　Méiyǒu.

④ 没有。

　　　Méiyǒu kè.

⑤ 没有　课。

⬥ 7. Do a report.

步骤：

(1) 学生读出每个课本上的课程名称。

(2) 学生总结一个星期内每门课程的节数，把得到的答案用星星代替画在每个课本方框后。

(3) 学生总结哪门课程的课节数最多。

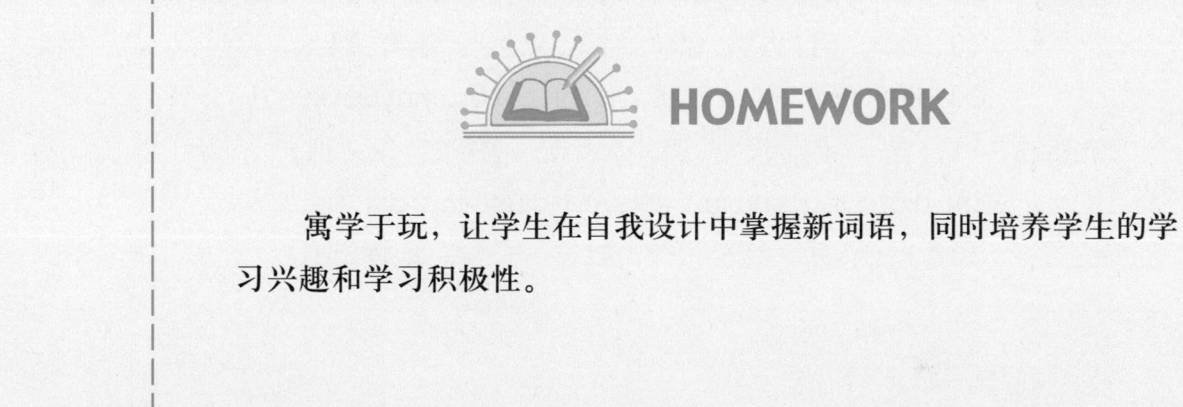

HOMEWORK

　　寓学于玩，让学生在自我设计中掌握新词语，同时培养学生的学习兴趣和学习积极性。

Lesson 8

我 在 上 网

交际话题：日常生活

教学目标： 句型：你在做什么？
我在上网。

生词：上网、睡觉、吃饭、洗澡、
报纸、作业、写、在、做

汉字：洗、澡

文化：中国小学生的课余生活

教学备品： （1）一个自制时钟。
（2）以前学过的有关小动物的道具（卡片或
者头饰）。
（3）爸爸、妈妈、方方等人物卡片和一些学
过的动词卡片如"看、写、吃、做、
玩"等。

STUDENT'S BOOK

复习与导入

(1) 学生展示图画——教科书封面设计，并讲解自己的设计思路。选出优秀作品贴在黑板上展示。

(2) 教师随意拿起学生的文具，向学生询问文具的价格，以复习上一课内容。

(3) 教师拿出时钟，拨到当下时刻，问学生"现在几点？"然后用英语询问"What are you doing now?"学生回答"We're having class."以此引出本课话题。

◆ 1. Can you say? (CD)

会话译文

What are *you doing*?

I am *going on the internet*.

替换部分译文

① *have dinner*　　② *read a newspaper*　　③ *sleep*

④ *have a shower*　　⑤ *do homework*

补充词

洗脸	xǐ liǎn	wash one's face
刷牙	shuā yá	brush one's teeth
打电话	dǎ diànhuà	make a call
做饭	zuò fàn	cook

游戏：

本课的生词有一部分是动宾词组，教师可将练习重点放在动宾词组的搭配练习上。

步骤：

(1) 教师拿出准备好的动词卡片，如"看""写""吃""做""玩""打"等，将其贴在黑板上。

(2) 学生思考并寻找可以搭配在这些动词后边的宾语。

(3) 学生A到黑板前，拿起自己知道的动词，举起来，并大声说出相关的动宾搭配。

(4) 教师把正确的答案写在黑板上，并做领读训练，以便于学生充分掌握。

句型讲解：

我<u>在</u>上网。

"在"是副词，表示一个动作正在进行，用在谓语动词的前边。动作进行的时间可以是现在、过去或将来。"正在"和"正"同样表示动作正在进行。此类句子的末尾可加上"呢"，形成"在……呢"或"正在……呢"格式。如：

我在写作业。

小王在唱歌儿呢。

他正在吃饭呢。

◆ 2. Can you try?

步骤：

(1) 学生分成四人一组，模拟一个家庭，其中一个学生作为旁白，手拿一只时钟报时，其他三个学生分别扮演爸爸、妈妈和孩子。

(2) 每组学生表演的内容包括：旁白选三个时刻，分别为上午、下午、晚上的某个时间。在每一时刻，家庭成员分别做不同的活动。比如把时钟拨到下午6点，问全体学生"现在几点？"学生们做出回答。

(3) 旁白学生问："爸爸在做什么？"扮演爸爸的学生立刻边做动作边做相应回答："爸爸在看电视。"旁白学生再分别问："妈妈在做什么？""你在做什么？"扮演妈妈和孩子的学生同上，边做边回答。

▲▼ 3.Let's talk. (CD)

步骤：

  （1）教师进行人物介绍：杰克、妈妈，翻译并讲解对话。
  （2）学生听录音，分角色朗读。 分组进行模仿表演。

译文：

  Mum: What's the time?

  Jack: 9 o'clock in the evening.

  Mum: What's your younger brother doing?

  Jack: He's taking a bath.

  Mum: How about your elder brother and elder sister?

  Jack: They are doing their homework.

▲▼ 4.Do you know? (CD-ROM)

中国小学生的课余生活

  中国小学生的学习生活比较紧张，但他们的课余生活也很丰富。下午放学之后，他们常常根据自己的兴趣选择一些辅导班继续学习，比如参加书法、音乐、外语、体育、棋类学习班等等。除了上述的课余活动外，他们也喜欢看电视、动画片，上网，玩儿电子游戏等。

  春天和秋天学校还会举行大规模的全校运动会、歌咏比赛、春游、秋游等活动，这些都是学生们很向往的。

▲▼ 5. Learn to read. (CD,CD-ROM)

▲▼ 6. Learn to write. (CD-ROM)

氵（水）

  部首"氵"是由"水"字发展变化而来（见学生用书1B第十一课讲解），凡带此部首的字都与水有关系。如汉字"江、河、湖、海、汁、泪(tear)"等。

故事内容:

中国人喜欢用四字成语表达自己的看法和观点,很多成语都用与动物有关的小故事来打比方。今天就介绍一个与"虎"有关的成语。

Hú Jiǎ Hǔ Wēi
狐 假 虎 威

一天,老虎在山林里捉到了一只狐狸,正要把它吃掉时,狐狸开口说道:"你怎么敢吃我呢?我可是天王派来管理所有动物的,你要是吃了我,天王会发怒的。"老虎不相信,狐狸又说:"你不信,可以跟在我后边走一趟,看看是不是所有的动物见我就逃。"老虎半信半疑地同意了。这样,狐狸大摇大摆地走在前面,后面跟着那只威风凛凛的老虎,一路上大大小小的动物果然吓得要命,四处奔逃。老虎看见了,不知道动物们怕的是自己,还以为是被狐狸吓跑的,就相信了狐狸的话,哪里还敢吃狐狸?

"狐假虎威"就是由这个故事得来的。现在,人们用它来比喻借着他人的权威,来使别人害怕自己。

步骤:

(1) 教师根据插图介绍故事内容。

(2) 学生准备道具,根据自己的水平可选择用汉语或英语表演。

(3) 在教师的指导下进行角色分配,并排练。

(4) 学生可进行公开演出,评选出优秀奖。

8. Story time. (CD, CD-ROM)

译文:

① What shall I do?

② Hello, I'm the teacher of the little rabbit. Tomorrow we'll have a maths test.

③ Thanks a lot.

④ Go home! Tomorrow you'll have a maths test.

⑤ Today we'll have a test.

WORKBOOK

1. Stick and write.

步骤：

(1) 学生试读拼音，猜测词义。

(2) 学生从不干胶贴页中找到缺失的部首，贴入田字格中，把两个字分别补充完整。

(3) 学生练写汉字，并查出每个字有几画。

2. Find and color them.

步骤：

(1) 学生看图找出正确的短语搭配。

(2) 学生把一个短语涂成相同的颜色。

答案：

shuìjiào/xǐzǎo/shàng wǎng/ kàn bàozhǐ/ xiě zuòyè

睡觉／ 洗澡／ 上　网／ 看　报纸 ／写 作业

3. Match them and say.

步骤：

(1) 学生看时钟确定时间。

(2) 学生根据词组内容连线，并为词组涂上喜欢的颜色。

答案：

shàng wǎng　　kàn bàozhǐ　　shuìjiào　 xiě zuòyè

①上 网　②看　报纸　③睡觉　④写 作业

4. What does Mingming usually do after noon?

步骤：

学生根据提示，填写明明正在进行的动作。

答案：

Míngming zài xué Hànyǔ.
① 明明　　在　学　汉语。

Míngming zài shàng wǎng.
② 明明　　在　上　　网。

Míngming zài xiě zuòyè.
③ 明明　　在　写　作业。

Míngming zài chī fàn.
④ 明明　　在　吃　饭。

Míngming zài kàn diànshì.
⑤ 明明　　在　看　电视。

Míngming zài xǐzǎo.
⑥ 明明　　在　洗澡。

Míngming zài shuìjiào.
⑦ 明明　　在　睡觉。

5. Listen, choose and color them. (CD)

步骤：

(1) 学生听录音，根据录音内容选择答案。

(2) 学生为正确动作的虚线图涂色。

录音文本：

Xiànzài wǔ diǎn, Nánxī zài xiě zuòyè.
① 现在　五　点，南希　在　写　作业。

Xiànzài qī diǎn, Ānni zài xǐzǎo.
② 现在　七　点，安妮　在　洗澡。

Xiànzài xiàwǔ sān diǎn, Jiékè zài dǎ pīngpāngqiú.
③ 现在　下午　三　点，杰克　在　打　　乒乓球。

Xiànzài wǎnshang bā diǎn, Fāngfang zài kàn bàozhǐ.
④ 现在　　晚上　八　点，　方方　在　看　报纸。

答案：①B　②C　③A　④A

▼ 6. Look , say and act it out.

步骤：

(1) 学生看图，根据图画内容逐一说出动物们此刻的动作。

(2) 学生利用小动物道具进行模仿表演。

答案：

① Xióngmāo zài chī fàn.
熊猫　　在　吃　饭。

② Mǎ zài hē shuǐ.
马　在　喝　水。

③ Tùzi zài xǐzǎo.
兔子 在　洗澡。

④ Māo zài shuìjiào.
猫　在　睡觉。

⑤ Xiǎoniǎo　zài chàng gēr.
小鸟　　在　唱　歌儿。

⑥ Jīnyú　zài yóuyǒng.
金鱼　在　游泳。

▲ 7. Interview your classmates.

步骤：

(1) 学生看图，读问题，采访周围的同学。

(2) 学生将提问每个问题得到的三个答案分别写在横线上。

HOMEWORK

学生根据本课的学习内容画一张特定时刻的家庭活动图，并向全班同学进行介绍。

Lesson 9

书 店 怎 么 走

交际话题：交通

教学目标：句型：请问，书店怎么走？
　　　　　　　　往左走。
　　　　　生词：前、后、左、右、书店、请问、
　　　　　　　　怎么、往、走
　　　　　汉字：左、右
　　　　　文化：中国的交通

教学备品：(1) 交通标记牌：红灯、绿灯或停、行。
　　　　　　(2) 用于捉迷藏的蒙眼巾。

复习与导入

（1）教师让学生分别拿着自己的作业为大家讲解在某一时刻，自己的家人分别在做什么。

（2）教师假扮一个路人或游客，问学生："Excuse me, how do I get to the bookstore?"并在黑板上画上方向标，让学生说出方向，引出本课话题。

◆ 1. Can you say? (CD)

教师根据课文插图进行讲解，同时在黑板上标出前、后、左、右，再引领学生分别标出本市书店、学校、医院、超市、公园等几处标志性的建筑，然后按本课句型提问学生，让学生回答方向。

会话译文

Excuse me, how do I get to the *bookstore*?

Turn to the *left*.

替换部分译文

① *park* ② *school* ③ *station* ④ *forward* ⑤ *left* ⑥ *right*

补充词

东	dōng	east
西	xī	west
南	nán	south
北	běi	north
警察	jǐngchá	policeman

句型讲解：

（1）请问，书店怎么走？

"请问"是敬辞，表示礼貌的请求，用于询问，置于句首。如：

请问，超市怎么走？

请问，你会汉语吗？

"怎么"是指示代词，"怎么+动词"用来询问动作的方式。如：

这个字怎么写？

你怎么来的？

(2) 往左走。

"往"，介词，表示动作的方向，跟处所名词或名词性词组组成介词词组，用在动词前。如：

往右看。

往前走。

◆ 2. Can you try?

步骤：

(1) 教师带领学生到操场上，在地上画出大坐标，标示出前、后、左、右。

(2) 教师把学过的表示场所的名词卡片（如学校、医院等），分别贴在一些学生背后。

(3) 这些背后贴有场所词的学生在大坐标上分别站好位置。

(4) 教师问其他学生："××怎么走？"学生们根据代表场所学生的站位齐声回答："往×走。"

◆ 3.Let's talk. (CD)

步骤：

(1) 教师介绍人物：警察、安妮、妹妹，翻译讲解对话。

(2) 学生听录音，分角色朗读并进行模仿练习。

(3) 学生分组表演，奖励优秀。

译文：

Annie: Look! "Stop when the red light is on, and walk when the green light is on."

Annie: Excuse me, how do I get to the station?

Policeman: Turn to the right.

Annie: Thank you!

4.Do you know? (CD-ROM)

中国的交通

中国的交通工具种类丰富，有公共汽车、地铁、电车、出租车、小汽车、自行车等等。中国是人口大国，对大多数人来说，最重要的交通工具还是自行车。在中国，几乎每个家庭都有自行车。到了上、下班的交通高峰时间，有些城市的主要街道几乎变成了自行车的海洋。随着生活水平的提高，越来越多的家庭开始拥有小汽车。中国的交通规则是车辆靠右侧通行，城市的交通路口设有红绿灯，而且还有交通警察维持秩序，为大家提供帮助。

5. Learn to read. (CD,CD-ROM)

6. Learn to write. (CD-ROM)

7. Let's do it. (CD-ROM)

捉迷藏游戏：红灯停，绿灯行

步骤：

(1) 户外，教师领学生们画一个10米见方的大方框。

(2) 学生们站在方框中，用"石头、剪刀、布"的游戏选出一个人，把这个人的眼睛蒙上。

(3) 这个蒙着眼睛的学生发令"绿灯行"时，其他学生可在框中随意走动。当他发令"红灯停"时，所有学生必须立刻停下，保持静止状态。若有人没停下来，被视为犯规接受惩罚。

(4) 蒙着眼睛的人随意去捉其他人，捉到后必须通过触摸的方式说出被捉者的名字，如正确，由这名被捉到的学生继续蒙着眼睛去捉其他的人。游戏继续。

8. Let's sing. (CD,CD-ROM)

译文:

Go Traveling

Stop at the red light, and go on at the green.

In my car, I go traveling.

By ship, by plane

I go to Shanghai and Beijing.

Turn left and turn right,

I have good friends everywhere.

"Excuse me."

"Thank you."

"You are welcome."

I have good friends everywhere.

WORKBOOK

1. Add the missing parts to the characters.

步骤:

(1) 学生根据英文猜测字义。

(2) 学生为两个汉字填补所缺部件。

2. Say as quickly as you can.

步骤:

(1) 学生读坐标"前后左右",熟记于心。

(2) 学生从入口处开始,快速说出每个小箭头的方向。

3. Listen and stick.(CD)

步骤:

(1) 学生看街景图，翻开不干胶贴页。

(2) 学生听录音文本。

(3) 学生根据听到的内容选出适当不干胶画贴入。

录音文本:

Yóujú wǎng qián zǒu, túshūguǎn wǎng zuǒ zǒu, xuéxiào
邮局　往　前　走，图书馆　往　左　走，学校
wǎng yòu zǒu, shāngdiàn wǎng yòu zǒu, gōngyuán wǎng
往　右　走，商店　往　右　走，公园　往
qián zǒu.
前　走。

4. Find the way.

步骤:

(1) 学生读提示对话。用手指或笔顺着入口方向行进，找到书店。

(2) 学生判断往左或往右走，填入对话空白处。

答案:

Wǎng yòu zǒu.
往　右　走。

5. Color them and choose.

步骤:

(1) 学生读图，根据图义判断图画上应亮起的是红灯还是绿灯。

(2) 学生为两幅图的指示灯涂上颜色，并将正确的选项填在图下括号内。

答案:

① B　② A

6. Find three differences between the two maps.

步骤：

学生看图，找出三处不同并说出。

答案：

①红绿灯　②警察手势　③指向标

7. Answer the questions.

步骤：

(1) 学生看图，通过标识判断各建筑的位置。

(2) 学生看问题，根据图示回答。

答案：

Wǎng qián zǒu.
① 往　前　走。

Wǎng qián zǒu.
② 往　前　走。

Wǎng zuǒ zǒu.
③ 往　左　走。

Wǎng yòu zǒu.
④ 往　右　走。

HOMEWORK

学生结合实际情况采访同学，以学校为出发点，完成去不同处所的指向表格。

UNIT FIVE TRAFFIC & TRAVEL

Lesson 10

我们坐飞机去旅行

交际话题：旅行

教学目标：句型：我们坐飞机去旅行。
生词：飞机、火车、汽车、轮船、自行车、
坐、骑、旅行
汉字：火、车
文化：中国主要的旅游城市

教学备品：(1) 中国旅游地图，风景名胜图片，如天安门、
兵马俑等。
(2) 交通工具模型。
(3) 彩笔、折纸卡、曲别针。

STUDENT's BOOK

复习与导入

(1) 教师检查作业，以学校为出发点，分别找学生说出到书店、医院、邮局、商店、公园、超市怎么走，以此复习上一课的词语和句型。

(2) 教师用英语问学生"你们喜欢旅行吗？""你们去过哪些地方？"在黑板上列出地名，并询问"怎么去？"学生分别回答"坐飞机去。""坐火车去。""坐轮船去。"等等，教师引出本课话题"坐飞机去旅行"。

◆ 1. Can you say? (CD)

教师将从前学过的一些城市的图片分别贴在黑板上，然后拿出交通工具模型，先讲"这是上海，这是北京，我们在北京，我们坐飞机去上海。"边说边拿着飞机指向北京；接着选别的地方，拿火车、汽车、轮船等模型逐一领学生练习。

会话译文

We are traveling *by plane*.

替换部分译文：

① *by ship*　② *by train*　③ *by car*　④ *by bike*

补充词

出租车	chūzūchē	taxi
摩托车	mótuōchē	motorbike
开	kāi	drive

句型讲解：

我们<u>坐</u>飞机<u>去</u>旅行。

汉语中的连动句是指两个（或两个以上）动词（或动词性词组）一起构成谓语的句子。连动句中前后两个动词的关系有多种，本课介绍的是前一动词或动词词组表示后一动作的方

式。如：

他们坐汽车去学校。

我坐飞机去（上海）。

2. Can you try?

步骤：

(1) 教师带学生到户外。

(2) 教师选出学生喜欢的旅游目的地，用木棍把写着旅游目的地的卡片或城市图片支起，分别置于不同的位置。

(3) 教师把学生分成五人一组，并要求每组的五个学生站成紧密的一排，不得走散或分开。

(4) 教师大声说出句子，如"坐飞机去上海。"学生立刻根据句义模拟该交通工具的姿势与声音开往目的地，看哪一组最先开到。

(5) 表现得又快又整齐的小组获得小彩贴。

3. Let's talk. (CD)

步骤：

(1) 学生听录音，分角色朗读并进行模仿、替换练习。

(2) 学生分组表演，奖励优秀。

译文：

Jack: I want to go traveling.

Annie: Where will you go?

Jack: Beijing and HongKong.

Annie: How will you get there?

Jack: I will get there by train.

4. Do you know? (CD-ROM)

中国主要的旅游城市

中国的旅游资源非常丰富，名胜古迹和自然景观遍布各地。下面介绍几个中国著名的旅游城市。

北京是文化古城，也是中国的政治、经济、文化中心，名胜古迹众多，有长城、故宫、颐和园、天坛、圆明园、明十三陵等世界著名的文化遗产。

上海是经济发达的现代化大都市，有外滩、东方明珠等著名景点。

哈尔滨是北方旅游名城，夏季气候凉爽，冬季则以冰雪天地、滑雪运动、冰灯节、冰雕节而著称。

西安是六朝古都，是中国最古老的城市之一，有兵马俑、华清池、大雁塔、华山等古迹和名胜。

香港是中国的特别行政区之一，也是世界金融、贸易、商业中心，是购物、游览、观光的著名城市。

苏州和杭州都是江南名城，以园林建筑和水乡特色而闻名于世，盛产丝绸和茶叶。

▲▼ 5. Learn to read. (CD,CD-ROM)

▲▼ 6. Learn to write. (CD-ROM)

火

本义指火焰。甲骨文的"火"字，像火苗正在燃烧的样子。汉字中由"火"组成的字大都与火有关，如灯（lamp or light）、烧（bur）等。

车

甲骨文中的"车"是一辆马车之形。以"车"为部首的字大都与车有关，如"轮（wheel）、转（revolve）、军（troops）"等。

▲▼ 7. Let's do it. (CD-ROM)

折纸游戏：飞机

步骤：

（1）让学生准备彩纸两张。

（2）练习折纸飞机：一种为传统折法，另一种为新折法，如图示。

（3）带领学生到户外，举行放飞比赛，看哪一种飞机飞得更高更快。

8. Story time. (CD,CD-ROM)

译文：

① We are going to the park!

② Excuse me, how do I get to the park? Turn left.

③ Excuse me, how do I get to the park?Turn left.

④ We want to go to the park, too!

⑤ Don't worry! Look, it's blowing!

⑥ We are going to the park by plane!

WORKBOOK

1. Write.

步骤：

(1) 学生看图，把虚线汉字描实。

(2) 学生读生词，说出词义。

2. Match them.

步骤：

(1) 学生看第一列图并读出英文。

(2) 学生根据词义进行连线。

3. Draw and write.

步骤：

(1) 学生在教师引导下说出每幅图的背景。

(2) 教师提问不同背景应配以哪种交通工具最合适。

(3) 学生画图。

(4) 学生将该交通工具的拼音填在空格内。

4. Listen and stick.

步骤：

(1) 学生打开不干胶贴页找到适当部分。

(2) 学生听录音。根据内容选择适当的不干胶贴画贴入圆圈中。

录音文本：

	Xiǎolóng	zuò	fēijī	qù	Měiguó.
①	小龙	坐	飞机	去	美国。

	Fāngfang	zuò	lúnchuán	qù	Xiānggǎng.
②	方方	坐	轮船	去	香港。

	Jiékè	zuò	huǒchē	qù	Shànghǎi.
③	杰克	坐	火车	去	上海。

	Gēge	qí	zìxíngchē	qù	xuéxiào.
④	哥哥	骑	自行车	去	学校。

	Ānni	zuò	qìchē	qù	shāngdiàn.
⑤	安妮	坐	汽车	去	商店。

5. A race.

步骤：

(1) 教师领学生朗读每个人物分别乘坐什么交通工具去香港。

(2) 学生判断出这四种交通工具从上海到香港的先后顺序并标出。

6. Read and say.

步骤：

(1) 学生朗读这些地名。

(2) 教师用汉语问学生到这些地方"怎么去？"

(3) 学生分别说出自己选择什么交通工具到什么地点。

7. Compose a dialogue.

步骤：

(1) 学生看图，根据图义，选择适当的句子，填入空白处。

(2) 学生分为两人一组，结合图中的对话情节试练习对话。

参考对话：

Xiǎolóng, nǐ hǎo!
Jack: 小龙， 你 好!

Nǐ hǎo!
小龙: 你 好!

Nǐ yào qù nǎr?
Jack: 你 要 去 哪儿?

Wǒ yào qù Xiānggǎng . Nǐ ne?
小龙: 我 要 去 香港。 你 呢?

Wǒ yào qù Běijīng.
Jack: 我 要 去 北京。

Nǐ zěnme qù?
Jack: 你 怎么 去?

Wǒ zuò lúnchuán qù .
小龙: 我 坐 轮船 去。

Wǒ zuò huǒchē qù.
Jack: 我 坐 火车 去。

HOMEWORK

绘图游戏：

　　教师让学生设计未来的交通工具（汽车或飞机）并在课堂上讲解其优越性，借此培养学生的想象力和独立表达能力。

UNIT SIX BIRTHDAY & FESTIVALS

Lesson 11

生 日 快 乐

交际话题： 祝贺生日

教学目标： 句型：生日快乐！
爸爸送我一个礼物。
生词：生日、蛋糕、礼物、手表、娃娃、
杯子、生日卡、快乐、送、个
汉字：快、乐
文化：十二生肖

教学备品： (1) 做生日帽所需的硬纸、彩笔、剪刀、胶
水等。
(2) 杯子、娃娃、手表等实物。
(3) 生日卡。

STUDENT'S BOOK

复习与导入

（1）教师让学生展示自己设计的未来交通工具图，并用英语说明其优越性。

（2）假设学生A今天过生日，教师拿出生日卡一张，说"生日快乐！"引出本课话题——祝贺生日。

1. Can you say? (CD)

会话译文

It's my birthday today. *Daddy* gave me a *gift*.

Happy birthday!

替换部分译文

① *mum, cake*　② *sister, cup*　③ *brother, watch*

④ *Annie, doll*　⑤ *Jack, birthday card*

补充词

晚会	wǎnhuì	evening party
蜡烛	làzhú	candle
眼镜	yǎnjìng	glasses

句型讲解:

（1）爸爸送我一个礼物。

这是一个双宾语句。在汉语里，少数及物动词后边可以带两个宾语，前一个叫间接宾语，多由指人的名词、代词充当；后一个叫直接宾语，多由指事物的名词或词组充当。如：

哥哥送我一个篮球。

妈妈送我一个手表。

"个"是量词，一般用于没有专用量词的事物。如：

一个人　一个本子　一个西瓜　一个汉堡包

(2) 生日快乐!

这个祝福语是"祝你生日快乐!"的省略形式，用来表示过
生日时的问候和祝福。其他类似的祝福语有：

新年快乐!

春节快乐!

2. Can you try?

步骤：

(1) 教师将学生分组，每组五人，一个扮小寿星，另外四人扮成朋友。

(2) 小寿星在一张卡片上写下自己的生日，四个朋友分别在卡片
上画出自己要送的礼物，准备参加生日晚会。

(3) 表演开始，小寿星出场举卡片说"今天×月×号，是我的生
日。"四个朋友同时出场，说"生日快乐! "小寿星说"谢谢。"

(4) 四个朋友逐一送上自己画的卡片，并说"我送你一个××。"

(5) 小寿星把收到的礼物卡片一一展示给大家看，同时说"××
送我一个××，××送我一个××。"

(6) 每组准备10分钟，表演后教师评优。

3. Let's talk. (CD)

步骤：

(1) 学生听录音，分角色进行模仿对话。

(2) 学生分组上台表演，教师讲评。

译文：

Annie: Today is my birthday.

Fangfang: Happy birthday.

A gift for you.

Annie: It's a doll!

It's very beautiful! Thanks!

▲ 4.Do you know? (CD-ROM)

十二生肖

古代中国人用十天干和十二地支相配来表示时间，同时又用十二种动物代表地支，用来表示人的出生年。这十二种动物是鼠、牛、虎、兔、龙、蛇、马、羊、猴、鸡、狗、猪。为什么要选用这十二种动物呢？说法有很多，其中一个传说很有趣，现在讲给大家听。

传说远古时没有纪年方式，玉皇大帝决定在他生日那天在动物中举行一场赛跑比赛，用最早到的12种动物名字来命名年份。那时猫、鼠是朋友，他们怕早上睡过头，就一起求助早起的牛叫醒他们。比赛当天一大早，牛让猫、鼠都跳到他的身上参加比赛，过河时老鼠趁机把睡着了的猫推下水，又在冲过终点时一下跳到牛的前面，于是成了第一，牛屈居第二，虎第三，兔第四，而本应跑得最快的龙因为去东方降雨迟到，成了第五，之后就是蛇、马、羊、猴、鸡、狗、猪。沉睡之中被推下水的猫什么也没得到，于是和老鼠成了世仇。生肖每十二年重复一次，你可以根据课本中的纪年表推算出自己和家人的生肖呢！

▲ 5. Learn to read. (CD,CD-ROM)

▲ 6. Learn to write. (CD-ROM)

▲ 7. Let's do it. (CD-ROM)

做一个彩色生日帽

步骤：

① 准备硬纸、胶水、彩笔等。

② 把一张长方形硬纸卷成圆锥形，在头上试戴一下，看看开口的大小是否合适。

③ 把纸卷用胶水固定粘牢，然后用彩笔画上喜欢的图案，也可以在帽边粘贴上小彩条，就得到了一个生日帽。

8. Let's sing. (CD, CD-ROM)

译文：

Happy Bithday

Happy birthday to you,

Happy birthday to you,

Happy birthday to you,

Happy birthday to you.

WORKBOOK

1. Write.

步骤：

（1）学生试读， 根据所给的笔画顺序，在后面框格内把虚线描实。

（2）学生查出每个字有几画。

2. Listen and color them. (CD)

步骤：

（1）学生看图，读出图片所代表的词语。

（2）学生听录音，选择。

（3）学生为选择的画儿涂色。

录音文本：

　　Bàba sòng　wǒ yí ge shǒubiǎo.

① 爸爸　送　　我　一　个　　手表。

　　Gēge sòng wǒ yí ge qiǎokèlì.

② 哥哥　　送　我　一　个　巧克力。

　　Jiějie sòng wǒ yí ge wáwa.

③ 姐姐　送　　我　一　个　　娃娃。

　　Māma sòng wǒ yí ge shūbāo.

④ 妈妈　　送　我　一　个　书包。

答案： 手表　快乐　杯子　蛋糕　生日　礼物

3. Look and write.

步骤：

(1) 学生看图，找出能组成词的汉字。

(2) 学生把生词写在横线上。

4. A maze.

步骤：

(1) 学生从入口处寻找正确通道，到达终点。

(2) 学生说出路上遇到的礼物，并说出礼物的名称，看谁说得最快最好。

答案：

dàngāo　shǒubiǎo　zìxíngchē

蛋糕　　　手表　　　自行车

5. Find out and say.

步骤：

(1) 学生看图，找到图中隐藏的各式礼物并抢答。

(2) 教师看谁说得最多，给予谁奖励。

答案：

máoyī　xié　qiǎokèlì　shǒubiǎo　shǔpiànr　wáwa

毛衣　鞋　巧克力　　手表　　　薯片儿　娃娃

bēizi　shū bǐ　shēngrikǎ　dàngāo

杯子　书　笔　　生日卡　　　蛋糕

6. Fill in the blanks.

步骤：

(1) 学生看图，理解图义。

(2) 学生根据段落大意填写所缺词语。

答案：

shí	yuè	wǔ	rì	shēngri	dàngāo	shūbāo	wáwa
10	月	5	日	生日	蛋糕	书包	娃娃

shēngrikǎ   hǎokàn

生日卡   好看

7.Design birthday gifts for your family.

步骤：

(1) 学生将家庭成员的生日标在日历上。

(2) 学生分别为他们设计一份礼物并画出图形。

(3) 学生说出送给家庭成员的礼物。

![HOMEWORK]

学生充分发挥自己的想象力，设计一张生日卡，送给要过生日的一个好朋友。

UNIT SIX BIRTHDAY & FESTIVALS

Lesson 12

新年快到了

交际话题 节日

教学目标：句型：新年快到了！

生词：春节、新年、圣诞节、爷爷、奶奶、
朋友、快、到

汉字：朋、友

文化：春节

教学备品：(1) 数字及月、日的卡片或一个日历。

(2) 月饼、饺子、火鸡、圣诞老人等图片。

(3) 一个红包。

STUDENT'S BOOK

复习与导入

(1) 教师让学生拿出自己给朋友制作的生日卡片，送给想送的同学，说：生日快乐！教师也可询问有无最近过生日的同学，组织大家一起为他唱生日歌。

(2) 教师拿出日历，翻到1月1日，用英语问学生这是什么日子，把答案"新年"用汉语写在黑板上，并引导学生说出"新年快乐！"同时，又把日历翻回十二月三十日，展开本课话题"新年快到了"。

◆ 1. Can you say? (CD)

会话译文

The *New Year* is coming . What are you going to do ?

I'm going to *travel*.

替换部分译文

① *Spring Festival,see my grandpa and grandma*

② *Christmas, see my friend*

补充词

感恩节	Gǎn'ēn Jié	Thanksgiving Day
中秋节	Zhōngqiū Jié	Mid-autumn Festival
儿童节	Értóng Jié	Children's Day

句型讲解：

新年快到了！

"快"是副词，表示时间上接近，很快就要出现某种情况，句末一般用"了"。"快……了"中间可加动词、形容词、名词、数量词等。本课学习"快+动词+了"。如：

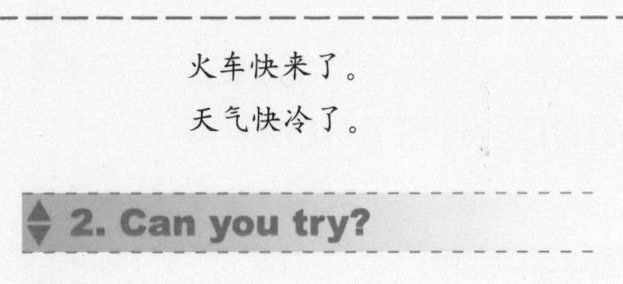

火车快来了。

天气快冷了。

2. Can you try?

步骤：

(1) 教师准备一本日历和本课学习的节日卡片，并制一张空白的统计表。

(2) 教师翻开日历，选择一个与本课所学节日（如新年）接近的日子，举起，问学生"今天几月几号？"学生根据日历回答。

(3) 教师接着拿出新年卡片领同学们说："新年快到了。"教师再问"新年你们想做什么？"学生回答。

(4) 教师把学生各种各样的回答写在统计表中并写出人数，然后得出学生在节日最想做的事。

(5) 游戏继续，教师接着用日历展示其他节日并继续提问。

3. Let's talk. (CD)

步骤：

(1) 学生听录音，分角色进行模仿练习。

(2) 学生分组上台表演，教师讲评。

译文：

Nancy: Spring festival is coming . What are you going to do?

Jack: I'm going to travel.

Nancy: When are you leaving?

Jack: On Saturday.

Nancy: How about Mingming?

Jack: He wants to see his friends.

4. Do you know? (CD-ROM)

春节

农历的正月初一，也就是农历新年，也叫春节，是中国最重要

的传统节日。"春节"预示着冬天即将过去，春天快要来临，人们祭祀天地、神灵、祖先，祈祷五谷丰登，万事如意。

春节是家人团圆的日子，人们无论在多远的地方工作，春节也都尽量从四面八方赶回家欢度节日。除夕之夜，人们有贴对联、吃饺子、放鞭炮的习俗，家家户户的门口都贴着大红的"福"字，到处都是喜气洋洋的节日气氛。初一早上开始，人们就开始互相拜年，互访亲友，小孩子不仅可以穿新衣服，放鞭炮，还可以收到长辈给的红包——压岁钱，他们是春节里最快乐的人！

5. Learn to read. (CD, CD-ROM)

6. Learn to write. (CD-ROM)

朋

古代的"朋"字表示"贝两挂"，用做货币计量单位，后指同一师门的人，现在指彼此有来往、有交情的人。

友

古代的"友"字像两只同时伸出来的手，两手相交表示握手，以示友好。"友"的本义就是现在的"朋友"，但在古代，"朋"与"友"是有区别的：同门为"朋"，即跟从同一个老师学习的人；同志为"友"，即志同道合的人才能称为"友"。

7. Let's do it. (CD-ROM)

手撕灯笼

步骤：

① 折纸 ② 画线 ③ 手撕 ④ 展开

8. Story time. (CD,CD-ROM)

译文：

① Tommorw is my birthday.

② So many gifts!

③ Mama and papa will be very busy today, so we'll not come home to eat supper.

⑤ Today is my birthday.

⑥ Happy birthday!

WORKBOOK

↕ 1. Write out the characters below the *pinyin*.

步骤：

(1) 学生读图和拼音，猜测词义。

(2) 根据词义填写汉字，查出笔画。

↕ 2. Match them.

步骤：

看图后，学生按每个人像找到相应汉字、拼音并连线。

↕ 3. Classify and stick.

步骤：

(1) 学生为春节、圣诞节两词涂色、说出词义。

(2) 学生把不干胶贴页上的物品按节日分类，分别贴在两个大框中。

答案：

① 饺子、红灯笼、福字、鞭炮、对联

② 圣诞树、圣诞老人、驯鹿、圣诞袜

↕ 4. Listen and fill in the blanks. (CD)

步骤：

(1) 学生看图，读问题。

(2) 学生根据录音文本将正确答案填入空白处。

录音文本：

Jīntiān   liù yuè   èrshí rì, xiàtiān   kuài dào le.

① 今天　　6 月　　20 日，夏天　　快　到　了。

Jīntiān   yī yuè   shíjiǔ rì,   Chūn Jié   kuài   dào le.

② 今天　　1 月　　19 日，春节　　快　到　了。

Jīntiān   shí'èr yuè   èrshíbā rì,   xīnián   kuài   dào le.

③ 今天　　12 月　　28 日，新年　快　到　了。

Jīntiān   shí'èr yuè èrshí'èr rì,   Shèngdàn Jié kuài dào le.

④ 今天　　12 月　　22 日，圣诞　　节快　到　了。

Jīntiān   jiǔ yuè shíliù rì,   qiūtiān kuài dào le.

⑤ 今天　　9 月　　16 日，秋天　　快　到　了。

◆ 5. Look and tell the differences.

步骤：

(1) 学生读两幅图，根据图中内容说出这两个节日的名称。

(2) 学生说出两个节日的异同，教师可组织学生先讨论后发言。
可用英语回答。

答案：

① 春节　　② 圣诞节

◆ 6. Interview your classmates.

步骤：

(1) 学生如图采访周围的同学，两个问题分别为：新年你想做什
么？什么时候去？

(2) 学生可用根据同学们的回答填表。

◆ 7. Color it and write.

步骤：

(1) 学生看图，根据教师提示选画笔。

（2）指导学生在气泡中填入祝福"春节快乐"。

HOMEWORK

学生画出自己喜欢的节日图，并在课上说明为什么喜欢这个
节日。

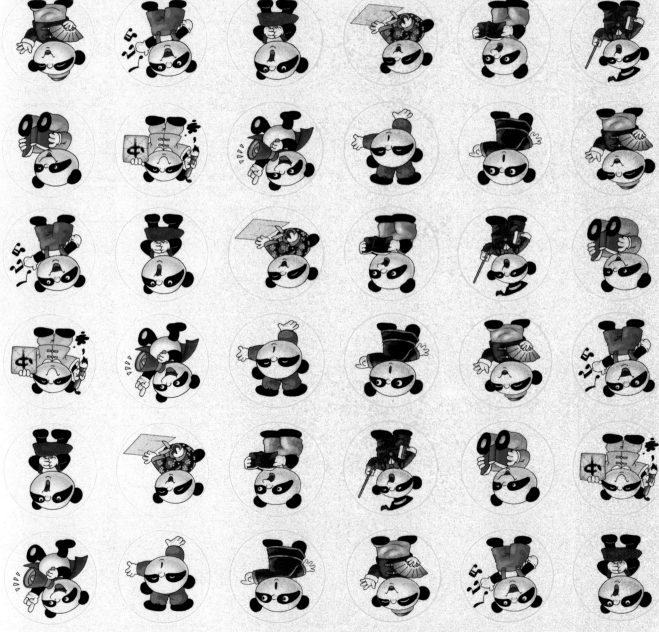